AWESOME VEGAN SOUPS

80 *Easy, Affordable Whole Food Stews, Chilis and Chowders for Good Health*

VANESSA CROESSMANN

creator of the blog Vegan Family Recipes

PAGE STREET
PUBLISHING CO.

PAGE STREET
PUBLISHING CO.

First published in 2017 by
Page Street Publishing Co.
27 Congress Street, Suite 105
Salem, MA 01970
www.pagestreetpublishing.com

Distributed by Macmillan, sales in Canada by The Canadian Manda Group.

21   20   19   18   17   1   2   3   4   5

ISBN-13: 978-1-62414-417-2
ISBN-10: 1-62414-417-9

Library of Congress Control Number: 2017936161

Cover and book design by Page Street Publishing Co.
Photography by Vanessa Croessmann

Printed and bound in the United States

As a member of 1% for the Planet, Page Street Publishing protects our planet by donating
to nonprofits like The Trustees, which focuses on local land conservation. Learn more at
onepercentfortheplanet.org.

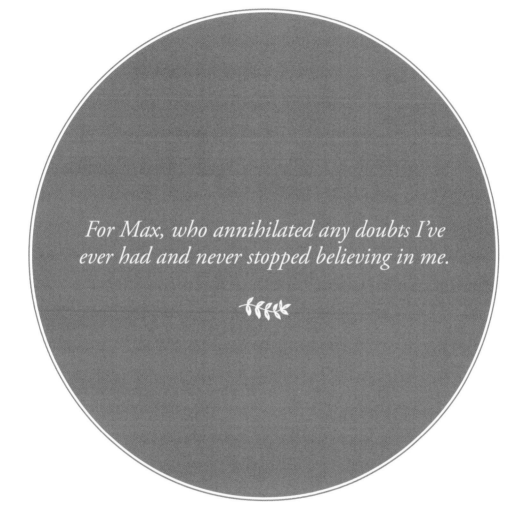

*For Max, who annihilated any doubts I've
ever had and never stopped believing in me.*

CONTENTS

HEARTY AND WARMING AUTUMN SOUPS — 15

COZY AND FILLING WINTER SOUPS — 59

EXTRAS AND TOPPINGS — 179

BRIGHT AND FRAGRANT SPRING SOUPS 101

LIGHT AND REFRESHING SUMMER SOUPS 139

INTRODUCTION— WHY SOUP?

Soup is delicious, easy to make and cost-effective. Those are some of the main reasons why it is consumed by people of all ages, all around the world. Soup can also help with weight loss and is a powerful way to eat yourself healthy.

When your child has a stomach bug, where do you turn? For most parents, they turn toward soup; and they do so with good reason. Not just because soups are easy to digest, but also because they are nutrient-dense.

Soups that are full with a variety of different vegetables give you the ability to consume your whole day's quota of certain nutrients.

Getting creative with your recipe and introducing more vegetables and whole food ingredients is a great way to ensure that you're getting a great amount of:

- Minerals—Brussels sprouts are high in potassium.
- Vitamins—Broccoli is high in vitamin C.
- Healthy Fats—Avocado is a great topping for soups and chilis.
- Fiber—Bean soups will keep you feeling full longer.

Beta-carotene found in carrots is known for fighting infections by improving white blood cells. Quercetin is an antioxidant that is found in onions that helps with your heart health. Most broths are already made with these two ingredients—imagine if we broke down the health benefits of every single vegetable, herb, legume or grain in a traditional bowl of soup. You'd convert to eating soup daily for life.

If you're looking to lose weight, soup is a great starting point. Start your meal with a small bowl of soup, and by the time you get to your meal, you'll eat less. The reason for this is that soup has a high water content, which makes you feel fuller. Combine that with whole grains and legumes and you'll also stay full.

Aside from the health benefits, eating soup is an easy way to save money. I have two hungry boys, a husband and myself to feed. With just a handful of ingredients, I can make a large batch of soup. It's enough to fill us up, plus we have leftovers for the next day and a healthy lunch for my husband to take to work.

Sometimes I even make soups out of leftovers. Did you make too much corn on the cob for your barbecue? Use that to make a grilled corn soup. Soups can really be made with a variety of ingredients, even the ends of vegetables that didn't make it into your ratatouille.

Tips for Better Soup

Even though making soup is fairly simple, here are a few tips for better soup:

- Stock It—Take the time to make your own vegetable broth. It's not hard to do and I even have a recipe for you (page 187)!

- Smelly Sweat—Onions and garlic are soup staples for good reason. They offer an abundance of flavor and fragrance to soups. Allow the onions and garlic (and other veggies too!) to sweat before adding the broth or other liquids.

- Gentle Heat—Be gentle with the heat. Your soup shouldn't be vigorously boiling. Let it come down to a nice, soft simmer. Your vegetables will thank you.

- Double Duty—Sometimes the best thing you can do with soup is double the batch. The cook time is usually the same and you'll have lots of leftovers for the remainder of the week.

- Savvy Cook—Be aware of the different cook times for vegetables. A large piece of cauliflower will take longer to cook than spinach.

- Slightly Salty—Don't be aggressive with salt. Add a little at a time and taste test. If you are buying store-bought broth, buy low-sodium or dilute it with some water.

Soup Storing

Serving sizes can vary a lot, which is why I like to give the amount of soup the recipe actually makes. The variation depends on how long you've let the soup cook or the size of your vegetables.

Refrigerating

If you plan on eating the soup within the next three days, you can refrigerate it. Let the soup cool to room temperature before putting it in an airtight container/bag in the fridge.

Freezing

You can freeze soup for up to two months, which is great for busy people and families. There are a few things to keep in mind.

- Freeze the soup in smaller, useable portions.
- Don't use freezer containers that are too big for your soup. Freezer burn will occur much quicker with more air trapped inside.
- Label your soup with the name of the soup and the date.
- Don't freeze pasta soups.
- Let the soup chill first before freezing.
- Thaw the soup overnight in the fridge.

Immersion Blender vs. Blender

I am definitely a firm believer in the immersion blender. I might risk sounding like a salesman here, but if you plan on making soups on a regular basis, invest in a good immersion blender. You can find decent ones for less than $30. Look for ones with a stainless steel attachment. My mother had one with a plastic attachment that I ended up melting making pumpkin soup years ago. No, thank you!

You can blend your soup right in the pot with an immersion blender. It's much quicker and less of a mess.

That being said, if you need to use a blender to blend your soups, take some precautions. There is nothing worse than adding a tomato-based soup into a blender, pushing the button, blowing off the lid and seeing beautiful red splatter all over your kitchen.

The best way to avoid that is to let your soup cool slightly. Fill your blender about halfway with soup and use a towel to firmly hold on to the lid of your blender. Pulse a few times then remove the lid to let some of the steam out of the blender. Slowly work your way toward blending the soup. Repeat with the remaining soup until all is blended.

WHY YOU SHOULD EAT SOUP ALL YEAR ROUND

Soup is always in demand and the ways you can serve it is endless. You can keep it classic, twist a comfort dish into a stew or even serve it cold. However, we can all agree that soup is the most comforting in the colder months. Soup warms us from the inside and even our kitchens as we cook them. So it's understandable that many forget that there are great soups in the warmer months too.

During the summer, a lot of produce is at its peak. Serving chilled soups, chock full of fresh vegetables, is a refreshing way to get lots of nutrients at once. Plus it makes for some classy summer dining, or so I'd like to think.

Whole Food, Plant-Based Diet

All the recipes in this book follow a whole food, plant-based diet. There are many reasons why people follow this diet. Whether it's for weight loss, lifestyle change or environmental reasons, it's safe to say that there are plenty of benefits with eating a whole food, plant-based diet.

What is a whole food, plant-based diet?

A whole food, plant-based diet is a lifestyle choice where the only food you consume is fruits, vegetables, legumes, nuts, seeds, minimal oils and unrefined whole grains.

Eating a whole food, plant-based diet means that you do not consume meat or dairy. But there are many meat and dairy alternatives available for your consumption. Popular meat alternatives are tempeh, tofu and edamame beans, which are a great source of protein for your dietary needs.

All nutritional requirements for your optimal health can be naturally found in whole grains, legumes, nuts, seeds and fresh produce, except for vitamin B-12, which is found only in animal products. Thankfully, you can take a supplement for that.

The difference between a whole food, plant-based diet and veganism

Whole food, plant-based foods are always vegan. However, not all vegan foods are whole foods. To put it in a nutshell, someone who follows a whole food, plant-based diet is basically following a healthy vegan diet that stays away from processed foods.

Veganism is also a lifestyle and not just a diet. It cuts out all animal-derived and animal-harming products that include not only food but also clothing, furniture, cosmetics and toiletries.

The two aren't mutually exclusive. A lot of vegans follow a whole food, plant-based diet.

How to avoid processed vegan foods

More and more people are following a vegan diet, and companies have caught on and are taking advantage of it. It seems that each time I go to the grocery store, new meat and dairy alternatives are added to the shelves.

On one hand, it's great to have so many new options; on the other hand, they are highly processed and incredibly expensive.

A lot of people who are new to a plant-based or vegan diet reach for these items because they think they need to replace an animal-derived ingredient in a recipe with a vegan one. Layering a processed vegan cheese over your vegetable lasagna isn't any healthier than dairy cheese. Often times these products are even worse for your health and your wallet than their animal counterpart.

The easiest ways to avoid vegan processed foods is to pretend like they don't exist. I walk past the dairy-free ice cream and vegan frozen meal section the same way I do past the meat aisle.

As much as we sometimes like to pretend, we're not all perfect. If I do see myself reaching for a prepackaged food, I check the label and look for items that have five or less ingredients that I can actually read.

Some people may see having to avoid processed foods as a punishment. That is definitely not the case. Companies that make processed foods try to be as cost-effective as possible in making them. From a business standpoint this makes complete sense. Companies want to use the cheapest ingredients, have a quick and effortless production and sell the product at a high markup.

The companies are really the only ones profiting from these, and the consumers definitely take a hit.

By avoiding processed vegan foods, I see it as a way to give my body actual nutrients.

For example, I used to have a love for store-bought veggie burgers. That changed the minute I decided to try making my own. I made my own veggie burgers over and over again, experimenting with different herbs and spices. The store-bought veggie burgers taste like cardboard to me now.

The same goes for soup. Canned and prepackaged soup CANNOT compare to homemade soup. It doesn't matter if it's all-natural, organic or made with unicorn tears. It does not taste the way soup should.

Think about how you would approach buying ingredients for a soup. Most of us would reach for the highest quality raw ingredients we can find. I don't think I have to tell you that the companies making canned soup are not doing the same.

Benefits of eating a whole food, plant-based diet

There are so many ways that a whole food, plant-based diet can positively impact your health. Eating healthy really is the best gift you can give yourself.

- Reverse Illnesses—This may sound too good to be true, but studies have shown that eating a whole food, plant-based diet can actually reverse many illnesses. Illnesses such as irritable bowel syndrome, fibromyalgia and heart disease are the most common ones to see a tremendous turnaround.

- Improve Sleep—Eating a diet that is low in saturated fat and rich in fiber has been proven to improve sleep, which we all would love more of.

- Clear Skin—If you're looking for ways to have clearer skin, think of the benefits of what anti-inflammatory rich foods can do for your skin. Eliminating dairy will help with any dark circles under your eyes, kicking butter to the curb will prevent zits and increasing your water and fiber intake allows your body to digest easier and detox your body of any toxins on a regular basis. Hello beautiful!

- Weight Loss—Many people start eating a whole food, plant-based diet to lose weight. Guess what? It works! When you're on a whole food, plant-based diet, there is no counting calories. You're giving your body exactly what it needs to thrive.

- Prevent Heart Attacks—Do you have a family history of heart disease? One of the best benefits of eating a whole food, plant-based diet is that it has been proven to halt heart disease. By not eating animal products, you're able to shrink the cholesterol-clogged plaque in your arteries. This means cutting out dairy, eggs and all meat products. That's a small price to pay for an assurance that eating this way will most likely keep you from ever experiencing a heart attack.

- More Energy—Feeling fatigued? Eating a whole food, plant-based diet that is balanced will give you more energy if you choose to eat superfoods such as raw nuts, hemp seeds, berries and citrus when you notice your energy is beginning to deplete.

- Preserve Your Environment—By choosing to eat a whole food, plant-based diet, you're choosing to save the lives of animals. You're also choosing to support local farmers and not support the livestock greenhouses that are creating high gas emissions that are affecting the global climate levels.

- Less Likely to Become Sick—By choosing to eat a whole food, plant-based diet, you're able to eliminate the allergies that come with dairy, meat and gluten consumption. If for some reason, you develop an allergic reaction to a meal, figuring out the culprit will be much easier.

- Save Money—Once you have your spices, supplements and other whole bulk-size ingredients in your pantry, saving money is easy. A meal plan that is focused on fresh, in-season produce is cheaper than a traditional American meal plan that is filled with meat and processed foods. Also, knowing that most restaurants and fast food places are not whole food, plant-based diet friendly really keeps you accountable with cooking at home and not eating out.

Why Seasonal Produce?

Eating produce in season saves money. Pick up your local supermarket's weekly ad and check out their produce that is on sale—what do you see? Most likely you'll find that seasonal fruit and vegetables are on sale in your local stores. Why is this?

When produce is in season, the prices are at an all-time low due to the abundance of it. Everyone has it, and they need it gone in order to replace it with more.

Your local farmers market will be your best bet for getting locally-picked produce at a low cost if you shop at the end of the business week or day, when most shops mark down their produce for a quick sale.

Don't forget that seasonal produce can also be homegrown!

Eating produce in season helps support local farmers and the community. By eating seasonal produce that has been grown locally, you can help support farmers and their workers by purchasing produce through a local community co-op or farmers market.

Purchasing seasonal produce locally helps your community continue to thrive financially and allows farmers to continue growing high-quality produce through the seasons to come.

Additionally, by choosing to purchase seasonal produce locally, you're able to help cut down on carbon footprints and your produce is not contaminated by oversea or cross-country deliveries.

Eating produce that is in season is more flavorful. Ever notice that an apple in September is bigger and tastes juicier than an apple in April? Or that a strawberry in December is not as appealing as a freshly picked, fully ripened, velvety-red strawberry in May?

Seasonal produce is picked when the fruit or vegetable is fully mature, leaving you with the best, juicy, vibrant and nutritionally dense ingredient.

Eating produce that is in season offers variety. Meal planning can be quite the adventure when you base it around seasonal produce. Creating recipes with new ingredients allows your family to escape the boredom trap when it comes to meals.

Commit to cooking with seasonal foods and try to think outside the box. If you've never heard of a certain fruit or vegetable before, hop on over to Pinterest; type it in and become amazed at the hundreds or thousands of recipe ideas offered to you.

There are many benefits and reasons why you should eat produce that is in season. Outside of saving money, becoming healthier, supporting your community, eating tastier meals and growing your own organic produce, I can think of only one deeper reason why you should eat seasonal produce. The reason is your family. Think of the impact you're going to make on future generations by teaching them the benefits of consuming seasonal produce and involving them in the selection process at the farmers market.

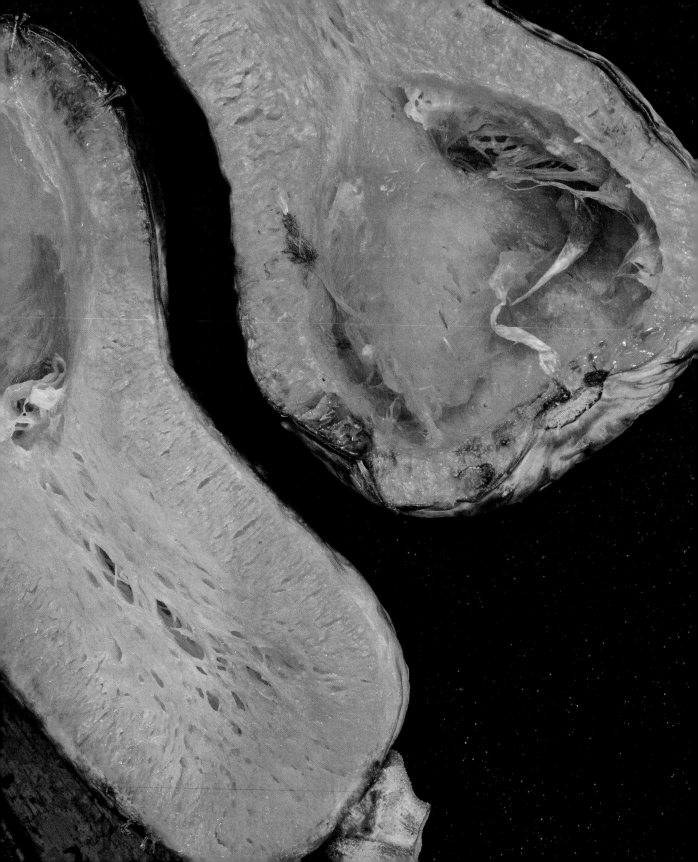

HEARTY AND WARMING AUTUMN SOUPS

Leaves change their colors in autumn and with it, the produce that is available changes as well. This is the time of year that has some of my favorite fruits and vegetables. For me, there is nothing quite as soothing as the velvety richness you get from roasting squash and pumpkin. The earthiness of mushrooms that are in abundance now can add a tremendous amount of flavor into one bite.

As the days get cooler, it's time to turn up the heat in the kitchen and make warm, comforting pots of soup. The recipes in this chapter are hearty and warming without feeling too heavy. If autumn had a specific flavor, it would taste like the Apple Pumpkin Soup with Chipotle (page 55). Be sure to give it a try!

WHAT'S IN SEASON

APPLES – BROCCOLI – CARROTS – CAULIFLOWER – CELERY – GINGER –
MUSHROOMS – PUMPKINS – PEARS – SWEET POTATOES – SWISS CHARD –
TURNIPS – SQUASH

MUSHROOM QUINOA CHILI

MAKES 3 QUARTS (2.8 L)

I've cooked lots of different types of chilis but this Mushroom Quinoa Chili is the one I like to make for friends and relatives who don't follow a plant-based diet. The chopped mushrooms have a similar texture to meat when cooked, which makes it great for new or non-vegans. The quinoa adds an extra protein boost and makes this chili recipe hearty, healthy and filling.

2 tbsp (30 ml) olive oil

1 large yellow onion, chopped

4 cloves garlic, minced

2 tbsp (15 g) paprika

2 tsp (5 g) cayenne pepper, optional–omit if you want a kid-friendly version

1 tbsp (2 g) dried oregano

1 tbsp (8 g) ground cumin

1 tsp smoked paprika

1 tsp salt

1 green bell pepper, diced

7 (100 g) cremini mushrooms, cleaned and chopped

3 Roma tomatoes, diced

4 cups (960 ml) tomato purée

8 cups (1.9 L) water

1½ cups (255 g) uncooked quinoa, rinsed

½ cup (120 ml) Vegan Sour Cream (page 180)

2 sprigs fresh cilantro

1 sliced cayenne pepper

Heat the olive oil in a large stockpot over medium heat. Add the chopped onion and cook for 5 minutes until it begins to soften. Add the garlic, spices, salt, bell pepper and mushrooms and cook for 10 minutes, stirring occasionally. Add the diced tomatoes, tomato purée, water and quinoa to the stockpot. Bring to a boil over medium-high heat. Once boiling, reduce the heat to low-medium heat and simmer for 20 to 30 minutes. The chili will thicken and quinoa will be cooked.

Pour the chili in bowls and serve hot with your favorite chili toppings such as vegan sour cream, fresh cilantro and cayenne pepper.

PER 1 CUP (240 ML) SERVING WITHOUT GARNISHES: CALORIES 150 ⫸⫸ FAT 4.2 G ⫸⫸ CARBOHYDRATES 25.2 G ⫸⫸ FIBER 4.4 G ⫸⫸ PROTEIN 5.3 G

NOTE

⫸⫸ I usually have chili leftovers. Chili always thickens when it cools, but this one does so even more because of the quinoa. When you reheat the chili, make sure to add anywhere from 2 tablespoons to 1 cup (30 to 240 ml) of water. The exact amount will depend on how much you are reheating.

SWEET POTATO CHILI

MAKES 3 QUARTS (2.8 L)

Sweet potatoes are inexpensive and delicious, and my kids love them.
Omit the cayenne pepper in this recipe to make this chili great for kids as well.

2 tbsp (30 ml) olive oil

1 large yellow onion, chopped

4 cloves garlic, minced

⅛ cup (15 g) paprika

2 tsp (5 g) cayenne pepper, optional

1 tbsp (8 g) ground cumin

1 tbsp (2 g) dried oregano

1 tsp smoked paprika

1 tsp salt

1 green bell pepper, diced, plus more for garnish

1 lb (454 g) chopped sweet potatoes

3 Roma tomatoes, diced

4 cups (960 ml) tomato purée

4 cups (960 ml) water

Vegan Sour Cream (page 180)

Fresh cilantro

Chili peppers

Chives

Scallions

Avocado, sliced

Heat the olive oil in a large stockpot over medium heat. Add the chopped onion and cook for 5 minutes until it begins to soften. Add the garlic, spices, salt, bell pepper and sweet potatoes and cook for 10 minutes, stirring occasionally.

Add the diced tomatoes, tomato purée and water to the stockpot. Bring to a boil over medium-high heat. Once boiling, reduce the heat to low-medium and simmer for 20 to 30 minutes until the chili thickens and the sweet potatoes can be pierced easily with a fork. Season the soup with more salt to taste.

Serve the chili hot with your favorite chili toppings such as sour cream, fresh cilantro, chili peppers, chives, scallions and avocado.

PER 1 CUP (240 ML) SERVING WITHOUT GARNISHES: CALORIES 119 ⫸ FAT 3 G ⫸ CARBOHYDRATES 22.8 G ⫸ FIBER 4.7 G ⫸ PROTEIN 2.9 G

AFRICAN SWEET POTATO PEANUT STEW WITH GINGER

MAKES 2 QUARTS (1.9 L)

I quickly became obsessed with this stew when I first started experimenting with it. The flavor profile works so well together. Each and every ingredient has a specific purpose, without overwhelming the other ingredients. Don't forget to squeeze generous amounts of lime juice over the stew at the end. It really takes the stew from tasting great to something you'll crave over and over again.

1 tbsp (15 ml) peanut oil

2 cloves garlic, minced

1 tsp grated, fresh ginger

2 tsp (5 g) ground cumin

¼ cup (60 g) tomato paste

½ cup (120 g) all-natural peanut butter (made from 100% peanuts is the best!)

½ cup (120 ml) water

1.4 lb (635 g) sweet potato, peeled

1 red bell pepper

1 carrot

4 cups (960 ml) vegetable broth

Cilantro

Raw peanuts

Fresh lime juice

Heat the oil in a large pot over medium heat. Whisk the minced garlic, ginger, cumin, tomato paste, peanut butter and water together to make a paste. Dice the sweet potato, bell pepper and carrot and add them along with the peanut butter paste to the pot. Stir constantly to prevent the peanut butter from sticking to the bottom of the pot, and make sure all the vegetables are coated well with the paste before adding the broth. Bring the stew to a boil then reduce to low heat and simmer, uncovered, for 20 minutes until the sweet potatoes are tender. Make sure to stir occasionally to prevent any sticking.

Garnish the stew with fresh cilantro and peanuts. Squeeze fresh lime juice over the stew just before serving.

PER 1 CUP (240 ML) SERVING WITHOUT GARNISHES: CALORIES 224 ⋙ FAT 10.7 G ⋙ CARBOHYDRATES 24 G ⋙ FIBER 4.5 G ⋙ PROTEIN 9.7 G

CURRIED CAULIFLOWER CREAM SOUP

MAKES 1 QUART (950 ML)

In high school, my best friend and I used to go to every Thai restaurant we could find. The only thing I would order was a vegetable red curry because why would you order anything else? This simple soup takes me back to my red curry obsessed days without requiring a whole lot of different vegetables and ingredients.

1 tbsp (15 ml) plus 1 tsp sesame oil, divided

2 tsp (10 g) red curry paste

2 cloves garlic, minced

½ head cauliflower (320 g), cut into florets

Small handful fresh basil, chopped, plus more for garnish

2 tsp (10 ml) fresh lime juice

2 cups (480 ml) vegetable stock

2 cups (480 ml) coconut milk

Salt and pepper

¼ cup (58 g) cauliflower, cut into small florets

1 cayenne pepper, sliced

Heat 1 tablespoon (15 ml) of sesame oil and the red curry paste over medium-high heat in a stockpot. Add the garlic and cook for 2 minutes until the garlic becomes fragrant. Stir in the cauliflower, basil and lime juice, setting some of the basil aside for garnish. Cook for 4 minutes then add the stock and coconut milk. Bring the soup to a boil, then reduce the heat and simmer for 15 minutes or until the cauliflower is tender. Purée the soup with an immersion blender, or in a blender, in batches. If the soup is not completely smooth, return to the stovetop and cook for an additional 5 to 10 minutes before puréeing again. Season the soup with salt and pepper to taste.

Heat the 1 teaspoon of sesame oil in a small frying pan and fry the cauliflower florets over medium-high heat for roughly 5 minutes, or until the cauliflower starts to brown. Add the sliced cayenne pepper and remaining chopped basil to the pan and fry for an additional minute.

Serve the soup hot with the cauliflower, basil and cayenne pepper as a topping.

PER 1 CUP (240 ML) SERVING WITHOUT GARNISHES: CALORIES 331 ≫≫ FAT 33.5 G ≫≫ CARBOHYDRATES 12.4 G ≫≫ FIBER 4.7 G ≫≫ PROTEIN 6.9 G

DAIKON GINGER MISO SOUP

MAKES 3 CUPS (720 ML)

If I have a cold, this is the type of miso soup I crave and need. The slight spiciness from the ginger and daikon clears my airways, and the miso soup is light enough to not make me feel heavy and groggy. Be aware that the longer the daikon and ginger steep in the soup, the spicier they will get. Miso soup is always best if eaten right away.

1 tbsp (2 g) wakame seaweed

2¼ cups (532 ml) water, divided

2 tbsp (40 g) vegan miso paste

⅓ cup (50 g) thinly sliced and peeled daikon

⅛ cup (10 g) chopped, fresh ginger

1 scallion, chopped

Soak the wakame seaweed for 5 minutes in ¼ cup (60 ml) of water to rehydrate it. Drain the water from the seaweed and set the seaweed aside.

Dissolve the miso paste in 2 cups (473 ml) of water. Bring the water to a boil in a stockpot, add the sliced daikon and ginger and remove the stockpot from the stove. Stir in the soaked wakame. Divide the soup into bowls, garnish with chopped scallion and serve immediately.

PER 1 CUP (240 ML) SERVING WITHOUT GARNISHES: CALORIES 40 ❯❯❯ FAT 0.9 G ❯❯❯ CARBOHYDRATES 6.6 G ❯❯❯ FIBER 1.5 G ❯❯❯ PROTEIN 2.1 G

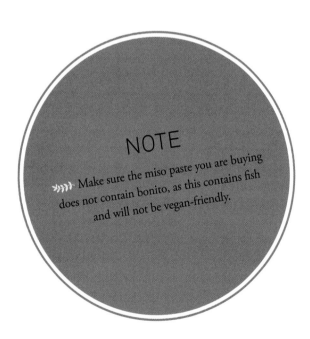

NOTE

❯❯❯ Make sure the miso paste you are buying does not contain bonito, as this contains fish and will not be vegan-friendly.

MIXED MUSHROOM STEW

MAKES 2 QUARTS (1.9 L)

A lot of the time, mushrooms are added to a dish as an afterthought. This stew really lets the mushrooms shine and shows off their rich and earthy flavor. From the picture, the stew also looks very heavy and creamy. However, it's actually quite light and balanced, making it perfect for lunch or a light dinner.

1 large carrot (roughly 120 g)

14 oz (400 g) mixed mushrooms

1 tbsp (15 ml) olive oil

1 small yellow onion, diced

2 cloves garlic, minced

1 tsp dried or fresh thyme

1 tsp dried or fresh rosemary

1 tbsp (15 ml) white wine vinegar

2 cups (480 ml) vegetable broth

1 (13.5-oz [400-ml]) can coconut milk

Salt and pepper

Parsley

Peel and dice the carrot. Brush any dirt off the mushrooms and chop into pieces. Set the mushrooms and carrots aside.

Heat the olive oil in a large pot over medium-high heat. Add the carrots, onion, garlic, thyme and rosemary and cook for 5 minutes until the garlic and herbs are fragrant. Add the chopped mushrooms, white wine vinegar, vegetable broth and coconut milk to the pot and bring to a boil. Once boiling, reduce the heat and simmer for 20 minutes, making sure the carrots are tender.

Season the stew with salt and pepper to taste and garnish with parsley before serving.

PER 1 CUP (240 ML) SERVING WITHOUT GARNISHES: CALORIES 172 »»»
FAT 14.2 G »»» CARBOHYDRATES 10.0 G »»» FIBER 2.9 G »»» PROTEIN 3.7 G

CREAMY ROASTED MUSHROOM SOUP

MAKES 1 QUART (950 ML)

Taking that extra step of roasting your mushrooms brings out the deep, earthy flavor mushrooms have. It's hard to not eat all the roasted mushrooms when they come out of the oven. However, they make for one super flavorful and rich soup that even my non-mushroom–loving kids enjoyed.

1 lb (453 g) cremini mushrooms, cleaned and quartered

2 tbsp (30 ml) olive oil, divided

2 cloves garlic, sliced

1 tsp salt

½ tsp black pepper

1 tsp chopped fresh rosemary

1 tsp chopped fresh thyme

1 yellow onion, diced

1 cup (240 ml) almond milk

1 cup (240 ml) water

1 cup (240 ml) vegetable broth

Salt and pepper

Fresh parsley

Preheat the oven to 400°F (200°C) and line a baking sheet with parchment paper.

In a bowl, mix together the mushrooms, 1 tablespoon (15 ml) of olive oil, sliced garlic, salt, pepper, rosemary and thyme. Spread the mushroom mixture across the parchment paper and roast in the oven for 15 minutes. Remove the mushrooms from the oven.

Heat the remaining olive oil in a stockpot and add the onions. Cook the onions over medium-high heat for roughly 5 to 7 minutes. Add half of the roasted mushrooms, almond milk, water and vegetable broth to the stockpot and bring to a boil. Reduce the heat and purée with an immersion blender, or in batches in a blender, until smooth.

Season the soup with more salt and pepper to taste. Add the remaining roasted mushrooms to the soup and sprinkle with fresh parsley before serving.

PER 1 CUP (240 ML) SERVING WITHOUT GARNISHES: CALORIES 254 ⋙ FAT 21.9 G ⋙ CARBOHYDRATES 11.8 G ⋙ FIBER 2.9 G ⋙ PROTEIN 5.9 G

RED LENTIL SOUP WITH ROASTED GARLIC CHARD

MAKES 2 QUARTS (1.9 L)

This soup is surprisingly easy to make and comforting, and the crisp, garlicky roasted chard gives this red lentil soup an extra punch of flavor.

1 tbsp (15 ml) olive oil

1 yellow onion, diced

3 cloves garlic, minced

1 carrot, diced

1 red bell pepper, diced

2 tsp (5 g) cumin

1 cup (200 g) dry red lentils

4 cups (960 ml) vegetable broth

2 cups (480 ml) tomato purée

Salt and pepper

ROASTED GARLIC CHARD
6 leaves chard

2 tsp (10 ml) olive oil

¼ tsp salt

½ tsp minced garlic

Heat the olive oil in a large pot and cook the diced onion over medium-high heat for 5 to 7 minutes. Add the garlic, carrot, bell pepper and cumin to the pot. Stir and cook for 3 minutes. Add the lentils, vegetable broth and tomato purée to the pot and bring to a boil. Once the soup is boiling, reduce the heat and let it simmer for 25 minutes. Purée half the soup with an immersion blender or in a blender. The soup should still be slightly chunky. Season the soup with salt and pepper to taste.

To make the roasted garlic chard, preheat the oven to 450°F (230°C) and line a baking sheet with parchment paper. Wash the chard and shake off the excess water. Place the chard in a bowl, drizzle with the olive oil and add the salt and minced garlic. Lay the chard flat on the baking sheet and bake for 4 to 6 minutes. The chard should have crisp leaves and a tender stem. Cut the chard into smaller pieces or serve whole over the soup.

PER 1 CUP (240 ML) SERVING WITHOUT GARNISHES: CALORIES 181 ⟫⟫⟩ FAT 4.3 G ⟫⟫⟩ CARBOHYDRATES 26.3 G ⟫⟫⟩ FIBER 10.2 G ⟫⟫⟩ PROTEIN 11.1 G

SPICY POTATO PUMPKIN SOUP WITH HARISSA

MAKES 2½ QUARTS (2.3 L)

Harissa is a spicy, northern African spice blend. It can often be bought as a paste, but I like making a dry spice blend of it myself. Harissa is very versatile, and a small amount can get overwhelmingly spicy very quickly. Always start off using less of it and slowly add more until you get to your desired heat level.

1 tbsp (15 ml) olive oil

3 cloves garlic, minced

1 lb (450 g) potatoes

1 to 2 tbsp (15 to 30 g) harissa

1½ lb (675 g) deseeded and peeled pumpkin

2 cups (480 ml) vegetable broth

3 cups (720 ml) water

Salt and pepper

¼ cup (60 ml) Whipped Coconut Cream (page 180)

Cilantro

Paprika

HARISSA SPICE BLEND

2 tsp (5 g) cayenne powder

1 tsp paprika

2 tsp (4 g) garlic powder

2 tsp (5 g) ground cumin

2 tsp (5 g) ground coriander

¼ tsp salt

Heat the olive oil in a large pot and cook the garlic over medium heat for 2 minutes until it becomes fragrant. Make your own harissa spice blend by combining all of the ingredients. Peel and dice the potatoes and add them along with the harissa and pumpkin to the pot. Stir all the ingredients together and cook for 4 minutes.

Add the vegetable broth and water to the pot and bring it to a boil. Once the soup is boiling, reduce the heat and allow it to simmer for 30 minutes. Purée the soup with an immersion blender or in a blender until smooth. Add salt and pepper to taste.

Serve the soup hot with a dollop of coconut cream, fresh cilantro and a dash of paprika.

PER 1 CUP (240 ML) SERVING WITHOUT GARNISHES: CALORIES 85 ⟫⟫ FAT 2.4 G ⟫⟫ CARBOHYDRATES 14.2 G ⟫⟫ FIBER 3.1 G ⟫⟫ PROTEIN 2.7 G

SWEET POTATO BROCCOLI SOUP

MAKES 2.2 QUARTS (2.1 L)

Sometimes it's tough getting my toddler to eat broccoli. He loves sweet potatoes though, and this soup
lets me hide a whole lot of broccoli in a soup he easily devours.

1 tbsp (15 ml) olive oil

2 cloves garlic, minced

2 lb (900 g) sweet potatoes, peeled
and diced

7 cups (1.7 L) vegetable broth

5 oz (2 heaping cups [140 g]) broccoli
florets

Salt and pepper

¼ cup (60 ml) unsweetened almond
milk

Basil Walnut Pesto (page 181)

Heat the olive oil in a large stockpot over medium-high heat. Add the minced garlic
and diced sweet potatoes to the pot, and stir occasionally for 2 to 3 minutes until the
garlic becomes fragrant, then add the vegetable broth. Bring the broth to a boil, then
reduce the heat and simmer for 10 minutes.

Add the broccoli to the pot after the sweet potatoes have cooked for 10 minutes.
Cook for another 5 minutes until both the broccoli and sweet potatoes are tender.

Purée the soup using an immersion blender, or in batches in a blender, until the sweet
potatoes are smooth. Season the soup with salt and pepper to taste. Serve it with a
drizzle of almond milk and a dollop of basil walnut pesto.

PER 1 CUP (240 ML) SERVING WITHOUT GARNISHES: CALORIES 162 ⟫⟫ FAT 2.8 G
⟫⟫ CARBOHYDRATES 28.6 G ⟫⟫ FIBER 4.3 G ⟫⟫ PROTEIN 5.7 G

PUMPKIN LENTIL STEW

MAKES 2 QUARTS (1.9 L)

This is the type of hearty stew I need when I've had a long day, and I'm physically exhausted and incredibly hungry. You can use any type of lentils for this soup, but I prefer black beluga lentils. Beluga lentils don't fall apart or turn to mush as easily as red or green lentils. They are rich in fiber, iron and protein and contain the same antioxidants that are found in dark berries.

1 tbsp (15 ml) olive oil

1 yellow onion, diced

3 cloves garlic, minced

¼ cup (15 ml) chopped fresh parsley

1 cup (200 g) black beluga lentils (or other lentils of choice)

4 cups (960 ml) vegetable broth

2 ribs celery, diced

2 cups (270 g) peeled and cubed pumpkin

Salt

Chopped parsley, for garnish

Heat the olive oil in a stockpot and add the yellow onion. Cook the onion for 5 to 7 minutes over medium-high heat until it becomes translucent. Add the minced garlic and chopped parsley to the stockpot and cook for 2 more minutes until the garlic becomes fragrant. Add the lentils and vegetable broth and bring to a boil, then reduce the heat and simmer for 5 minutes. Add the diced celery and pumpkin and simmer for another 20 minutes.

Season the soup with salt to taste. Serve hot with more fresh parsley.

PER 1 CUP (240 ML) SERVING WITHOUT GARNISHES: CALORIES 130 ⇉ FAT 2.8 G ⇉ CARBOHYDRATES 17.6 G ⇉ FIBER 6.4 G ⇉ PROTEIN 9.1 G

AUTUMN VEGETABLE MINESTRONE

MAKES 2 QUARTS (1.9 L)

Minestrone is always a crowd-pleaser. It's also a great way to empty out your fridge of any excess vegetables you may have lurking about. I really like getting my kids involved when I make minestrone. I let them dig through the fridge and pick out which veggies they want to add and then which type of pasta. I've had to make minestrone before with three different types of pasta thanks to my toddler.

1 tbsp (15 ml) olive oil

1 yellow onion, diced

2 cloves garlic, minced

1 tsp dried basil

1 tsp dried oregano

2 carrots, diced

2 ribs celery, roughly diced

14 oz (400 g) sweet potatoes, peeled and diced

4 oz (115 g) deseeded and peeled pumpkin, diced

2 cups (480 ml) tomato purée

4 cups (960 ml) vegetable broth

1 bay leaf

1 cup (170 g) cannellini beans, soaked and cooked or rinsed and drained from a can

1 cup (116 g) uncooked whole grain small pasta (mini farfalle, elbows, pipettes, etc.)

Salt and pepper

Fresh basil

Heat the olive oil in a large pot, add the onions and cook for 5 minutes until they are translucent. Add the minced garlic, basil, oregano, carrots, celery, sweet potatoes and pumpkin. Cook the vegetables for 5 minutes, stirring often, then add the tomato purée, vegetable broth and bay leaf.

Bring the soup to a boil, then reduce the heat and simmer for 10 minutes. Add the beans and pasta. Cook until the pasta and all the vegetables are tender. This will vary depending on the type and size of the pasta.

Remove the bay leaf and season the minestrone with salt and pepper to taste before serving it with some fresh basil.

PER 1 CUP (240 ML) SERVING WITHOUT GARNISHES: CALORIES 303 ⫸ FAT 3.3 G ⫸ CARBOHYDRATES 55.9 G ⫸ FIBER 14.2 G ⫸ PROTEIN 14.4 G

LOADED SWEET POTATO SOUP WITH TEMPEH BITS

MAKES 1½ QUARTS (1.4 L)

This is a very simple and much healthier version of a loaded sweet potato soup. The tempeh bits add a delicious smoky flavor that works really well with the sweetness from the potatoes and pumpkin. I love using the leftover tempeh bits on other soups and salads. So good!

1 small yellow onion, finely diced

1 lb (450 g) sweet potatoes, peeled and diced

7 oz (200 g) deseeded and peeled pumpkin, diced

4 cups (960 ml) vegetable broth

Salt and pepper

Vegan Sour Cream (page 180)

Chives

TEMPEH BITS
5 oz (141 g) tempeh

1 tbsp (15 ml) liquid smoke

2 tsp (10 ml) soy sauce

1 tsp maple syrup

2 tsp (5 g) ground paprika

1 tsp olive oil

Add the yellow onion, sweet potatoes, pumpkin and vegetable broth to a pot and bring it to a boil. Once boiling, reduce the heat, cover and simmer for 15 to 20 minutes until the pumpkin and sweet potatoes are tender.

Meanwhile, prepare the tempeh bits. Crumble the tempeh with your fingers into little pieces. Mix it with the liquid smoke, soy sauce, maple syrup and paprika. Heat the olive oil over medium-high heat in a small sauté pan and add the tempeh to it. Cook the tempeh for roughly 3 to 4 minutes, stirring often, until browned. Remove the tempeh bits from the pan and set aside.

Once the pumpkin and sweet potatoes are tender, purée the soup using an immersion blender, or blend in batches in a blender, until creamy and smooth. Season the soup with salt and pepper to taste. Serve the soup in a bowl and top with vegan sour cream, chives and tempeh bits.

PER 1 CUP (240 ML) SERVING WITHOUT GARNISHES: CALORIES 162 ⟫⟫ FAT 3.6 G ⟫⟫ CARBOHYDRATES 28.2 G ⟫⟫ FIBER 4.6 G ⟫⟫ PROTEIN 6.2 G

CHICKPEA STEW WITH PUMPKIN AND CAULIFLOWER

MAKES 2 QUARTS (1.9 L)

I started making chickpea stew by accident. I used to throw a lot of ingredients in a pot and let it simmer until it seemed right to me. However, that method caused all my veggies (and especially my chickpeas) to have baby food texture. Fast forward to several years later, and I finally realized how to perfect my favorite chickpea stew without having my veggies and chickpeas become mush.

1 tbsp (15 ml) olive oil

1 red onion, quartered and sliced

½ tsp salt

2 cloves garlic, minced

1 tbsp (8 g) ground cumin

1 tbsp (8 g) smoked paprika

4 Roma tomatoes, diced

2 cups (270 g) peeled and cubed pumpkin

¼ (160 g) head cauliflower, cut into florets

3 cups (720 ml) water

2 bay leaves

3 cups (600 g) chickpeas, soaked and cooked or rinsed and drained from a can

1 tbsp (15 ml) fresh lemon juice

Fresh parsley

Heat the olive oil in a medium pot over medium-high heat. Add the sliced red onion and salt and cook, stirring often, for 3 minutes. Add the garlic, cumin and smoked paprika to the pot and cook for 1 more minute until the garlic becomes fragrant. Add the diced tomatoes, pumpkin and cauliflower and cook for 3 minutes, stirring often. Add the water and bay leaves, bring to a boil, then reduce the heat to medium-low and simmer, uncovered, for 20 minutes or until the pumpkin is tender. Add the chickpeas and lemon juice and cook for 5 minutes.

Remove the bay leaves and season the soup with more salt and lemon juice to taste. Serve hot with fresh parsley. The stew can be eaten alone or over couscous, quinoa or rice.

PER 1 CUP (240 ML) SERVING WITHOUT GARNISHES: CALORIES 253 ⟫⟫ FAT 5.7 G ⟫⟫ CARBOHYDRATES 40.7 G ⟫⟫ FIBER 12 G ⟫⟫ PROTEIN 12.5 G

MUSHROOM MISO SOUP

MAKES 3 CUPS (720 ML)

Miso soup is one of my favorite Japanese foods. Sadly, a lot of the miso soups at restaurants aren't entirely plant-based, as they often contain bonito (fish flakes). Luckily though, miso is incredibly easy to make at home. Just make sure that the miso paste you buy is vegan-friendly and without bonito.

1 tbsp (2 g) wakame seaweed

3¼ cups (770 ml) water, divided

1 cup (50 g) chopped mushrooms of choice (oyster, cremini, shiitake)

2 tbsp (40 g) miso paste

1 scallion, chopped, for garnish

Soak the wakame in a cup (240 ml) of water for 5 minutes to rehydrate the seaweed, then drain the water and set the wakame aside. Heat 2 cups (480 ml) of water in a small stockpot and bring it to a boil. Add the mushrooms to the boiling water and let them cook for 4 minutes.

While the mushrooms are cooking, dissolve the miso paste in the remaining ¼ cup (60 ml) of water. Remove the stockpot from the stove and stir in the soaked wakame and miso paste.

Divide the soup into bowls, garnish with chopped scallion and serve immediately.

PER 1 CUP (240 ML) SERVING WITHOUT GARNISHES: CALORIES 31 ⋙ FAT 0.9 G ⋙ CARBOHYDRATES 4.2 G ⋙ FIBER 0.9 G ⋙ PROTEIN 2.1 G

GARLIC PEANUT NOODLE SOUP

MAKES 2 QUARTS (1.9 L)

Let the noodle slurping begin! This noodle soup has all my favorite Thai flavors. Oh, and some peanut butter because we all need more peanut butter in our lives. It can be fairly messy to eat, but the flavors are worth it!

1 tsp sesame oil

3 cloves garlic, minced

½ tsp grated ginger

1 (13.5-oz [400-ml]) can coconut milk

¼ cup (60 g) red curry paste

⅓ cup (80 ml) natural peanut butter (best if made from 100% peanuts)

3 cups (720 ml) vegetable broth

2 cups (480 ml) water

¼ cup (60 ml) fresh lime juice

1 tsp turmeric

1 lb (450 g) sweet potatoes

2 cups (180 g) broccoli florets

¼ cup (40 g) unsalted peanuts, toasted and chopped

6 oz (170 g) brown rice noodles

1 cup (100 g) snow peas

1 scallion, chopped for garnish

Cilantro, chopped for garnish

Heat the oil in a large saucepan or wok, and add the garlic and ginger. Cook for 2 minutes over medium-high heat before you add the coconut milk. Whisk the red curry paste and peanut butter into the coconut milk. Then add the vegetable broth, water, lime juice and turmeric. Peel and dice the sweet potatoes before adding them to the saucepan. Bring everything to a boil, then reduce the heat and simmer for 15 to 20 minutes until the sweet potatoes are tender.

While the sweet potatoes are cooking, cut the broccoli into florets and dry roast the peanuts in a small pan for 2 minutes until they are slightly browned, then chop them.

Once the sweet potatoes are tender, add the broccoli, brown rice noodles and snow peas. Cook for 4 minutes until the broccoli is bright green and the noodles are tender.

Serve the soup immediately and garnish it with the peanuts, scallion and fresh cilantro.

PER 1 CUP (240 ML) SERVING WITHOUT GARNISHES: CALORIES 398 »»»
FAT 21.8 G »»» CARBOHYDRATES 42.1 G »»» FIBER 5.9 G »»» PROTEIN 10.1 G

THAI RED CURRY SWEET POTATO SOUP

MAKES 1 QUART (950 ML)

Spicy red curry and sweet potatoes—this is one of my favorite pairings.
The fact that this soup is also incredibly easy to make is just an added bonus!

2 tsp (10 ml) sesame oil

1 red onion, diced

4 cloves garlic, minced

2 tsp (10 g) minced ginger

2 tbsp (30 g) Thai red curry paste

2 cups (280 g) diced sweet potatoes

3 cups (720 ml) water

1 cup (200 g) coconut cream

Salt and cayenne pepper, to taste

Fresh cilantro, for garnish

Heat the oil in a stockpot and add the onion. Cook the onion for several minutes over medium-high heat until the onion becomes translucent. Add the garlic, ginger, curry paste and sweet potatoes to the stock pot and cook for 4 more minutes. Stir the water into the pot and bring to a boil. Once boiling, reduce the heat and simmer for 10 to 15 minutes until the sweet potatoes are tender. Stir in the coconut cream, bring to another boil and simmer for 10 more minutes.

Season the soup with salt and cayenne pepper to taste. Serve the soup hot with fresh cilantro and extra cayenne pepper.

PER 1 CUP (240 ML) SERVING WITHOUT GARNISHES: CALORIES 266 ⟫⟫⟫
FAT 16.7 G ⟫⟫⟫ CARBOHYDRATES 28 G ⟫⟫⟫ FIBER 4.7 G ⟫⟫⟫ PROTEIN 2.8 G

ROASTED APPLE BUTTERNUT SQUASH SOUP

MAKES 2½ QUARTS (2.3 L)

Simply boiling your produce won't always lead to explosively flavorful dishes. If you have a bit more time on your hands, roasting your apples and butternut squash will deliver a deep, sweet flavor that you otherwise wouldn't be able to coax out of them. Definitely worth the extra time!

½ butternut squash (680 g), seeds removed

2 tbsp (30 ml) olive oil, divided

2 apples, peeled, quartered and cored

1 yellow onion, diced

2 cloves garlic, minced

3 cups (720 ml) vegetable broth

Pinch of nutmeg

Salt and pepper

Pumpkin seeds, for garnish

Preheat the oven to 425°F (220°C) and line a baking sheet with parchment paper. Cut the butternut squash in half. Place one of the halves in the fridge for later use. Remove the seeds from the other butternut squash half and set aside. Rub 1 tablespoon (15 ml) of olive oil over the apples and butternut squash and place them on the lined baking sheet. The squash should be placed face down. Roast the apples and squash in the oven for 30 to 45 minutes until the squash is tender. Remove the squash and apples from the oven and allow them to cool for at least 10 minutes.

While the apples and squash are cooling, heat 1 tablespoon (15 ml) of olive oil in a large stockpot, add the diced onion and cook for 5 to 7 minutes over medium-high heat. Add the minced garlic to the stockpot and cook for another minute until the garlic becomes fragrant.

At this point, the squash and apples should be cool enough to handle. Add the apples to the pot and scoop the butternut squash flesh with a spoon into the pot. Discard the tough butternut squash skin. Pour the vegetable broth and nutmeg into the stockpot and bring to a boil. Purée the soup using an immersion blender, or in batches in a blender, until smooth.

Season with salt and pepper to taste and serve hot. Garnish with pumpkin seeds.

PER 1 CUP (240 ML) SERVING WITHOUT GARNISHES: CALORIES 95 ⇒ FAT 3.4 G ⇒ CARBOHYDRATES 15.6 G ⇒ FIBER 2.7 G ⇒ PROTEIN 2.4 G

CHICKPEA TURMERIC SOUP WITH SWEET POTATOES

MAKES 1 QUART (950 ML)

Turmeric has so many health benefits, but it is an ingredient I don't usually consume on a daily basis. This soup makes up for that by adding a lot of healthy ingredients together to make this rich, chunky and filling soup.

1 tsp sesame oil

1 small yellow onion, diced

2 cloves garlic, minced

2 tsp (10 g) minced ginger

1 tbsp (8 g) turmeric

1 tsp cumin

1 cup (240 g) chickpeas, soaked and cooked or rinsed and drained from a can

1 heaping cup (140 g) diced sweet potatoes

2 cups (480 ml) low-sodium vegetable broth, divided

1 tsp fresh lemon juice or more

Salt and pepper

Parsley, for garnish

Heat the oil in a stockpot and add the diced onion. Cook the onion over medium-high heat until it becomes translucent. Add the garlic, ginger, turmeric and cumin and cook for 2 more minutes. Add the chickpeas, sweet potatoes and ¼ cup (60 ml) of the broth to the stockpot and cook for 5 minutes, stirring often. Add the remaining vegetable broth, bring to a boil, then reduce the heat and simmer for 15 minutes until the sweet potatoes are tender.

Use an immersion blender or blender to blend the soup slightly so that the soup is chunky. Stir in the lemon juice, starting with 1 teaspoon and adding more according to taste.

Season the soup with salt and pepper to taste and serve hot with fresh parsley and more lemon if needed.

PER 1 CUP (240 ML) SERVING WITHOUT GARNISHES: CALORIES 225 ⇒ FAT 4 G ⇒ CARBOHYDRATES 40.1 G ⇒ FIBER 9.3 G ⇒ PROTEIN 8.9 G

If
m
wh

1 tbsp (15
1 clove ga
1 apple, pe
apple, but
like a sony
2 ribs cele
3 cups (40
pumpkin
2 cups (48
¾ cup (18
1 (7-oz [19
adobo sauc
Whipped (
for garnish
Small hand
for garnish

SPICY POTATO KALE SOUP

MAKES 2½ QUARTS (2.4 L)

This is such an easy and incredibly healthy winter stew to make. There are no fancy techniques necessary, making it the perfect stew when you just want to throw a bunch of ingredients in a pot and let it cook. Omit the cayenne pepper if kids will be eating this soup.

1 rib celery

1 large carrot (roughly 120 g)

15 oz (425 g) potatoes

3½ oz (100 g) kale

1 tbsp (15 ml) olive oil

1 small yellow onion, diced

1 cayenne pepper or ⅛ to ¼ of tsp dried cayenne pepper

1 tsp dried or fresh thyme

3½ cups (840 ml) vegetable broth

1 tbsp (15 ml) red wine vinegar

Salt and pepper

Peel and chop the celery, carrot and potatoes. Wash the kale and remove the leaves from the stems. Chop the leaves and discard the stems. Set the celery, carrot, potatoes and kale aside.

Heat the olive oil in a large pot over medium-high heat and cook the onion for 5 minutes. Add the cayenne pepper, thyme, celery, carrot and potatoes to the pot and cook, stirring occasionally, for 5 minutes. Add the vegetable broth and allow the soup to simmer for 10 minutes. Then, add the chopped kale leaves, letting them sit on top of the broth. As the steam rises from the cooking stew, the kale will slowly fall into the stew and cook. Cook for 10 minutes until the potatoes and carrots are tender.

Stir in the red wine vinegar, season with salt and pepper to taste and serve the stew hot. The longer you let the stew cook, the less broth will be left. If needed, you can add more water or broth.

PER 1 CUP (240 ML) SERVING WITHOUT GARNISHES: CALORIES 68 ⇒ FAT 1.9 G ⇒ CARBOHYDRATES 10 G ⇒ FIBER 1.7 G ⇒ PROTEIN 2.9 G

HUNGARIAN TEMPEH GOULASH

MAKES 2 QUARTS (1.9 L)

Traditionally, goulash is very meat heavy and even though I don't eat meat, I always find the smell of goulash delicious. So I desperately wanted a vegan version of goulash that smells just as good but tastes even better. The key to this vegan goulash is being very generous with the amount of paprika and smoked paprika you use. The more the better!

1 yellow onion

6 oz (170 g) tempeh

1 tbsp (15 ml) olive oil

1 tsp thyme

1 tsp rosemary

⅛ cup (13 g) paprika

¼ cup (27 g) smoked paprika

1 bay leaf

4 cloves garlic

2 large carrots

1 lb (450 g) potatoes

2 red bell peppers

2 Roma tomatoes

6 cups (1.4 L) vegetable broth

Salt and pepper

Vegan Sour Cream (page 180), for serving

Dice the onion and tempeh before heating the olive oil in a large pot over medium-high heat. Add the diced onion and cook for 5 minutes until it starts to brown. Add the tempeh, thyme, rosemary, paprika, smoked paprika, bay leaf and garlic and cook for an additional 5 minutes until the garlic and paprika become very fragrant.

While the spices are cooking, peel and dice the carrots and potatoes, slice the bell peppers and dice the tomatoes. Add the tomatoes, carrots, potatoes and bell peppers to the pot and cook for 5 more minutes, stirring occasionally. Add the vegetable broth and bring the goulash to a boil. Once the goulash is boiling, reduce to medium heat, cover and let it simmer for 40 minutes until the potatoes are cooked.

Remove the bay leaf and season the goulash with salt and pepper to taste. Serve with a dollop of vegan sour cream.

PER 1 CUP (240 ML) SERVING WITHOUT GARNISHES: CALORIES 169 ⇥ FAT 6 G ⇥ CARBOHYDRATES 22.5 G ⇥ FIBER 4.8 G ⇥ PROTEIN 10.2 G

ROASTED WINTER VEGETABLE SOUP WITH BULGUR

MAKES 1½ QUARTS (1.4 L)

Just the smell of these roasted veggies in the kitchen is enough to turn one of those dark winter days into one that's just a bit more pleasant. It's simple enough to make and the bulgur helps fill you up.

1 yellow onion

4 ribs celery

6 oz (170 g) parsnips

8 oz (225 g) kohlrabi

2 large carrots

12 to 15 Brussels sprouts

1 tbsp (15 ml) olive oil

1 tbsp (2 g) fresh chopped rosemary or 1 tsp dried rosemary

1 tsp fresh chopped thyme leaves or ½ tsp dried thyme

Pinch of salt

½ cup (70 g) uncooked whole grain bulgur

5 cups (1.2 L) vegetable broth

2 tsp (10 ml) or more balsamic vinegar

Salt and pepper

Preheat the oven to 425°F (218°C). Quarter the onion, slice the celery and dice the parsnips, kohlrabi and carrots. Rinse off the Brussels sprouts, remove the tip of the stem of each and remove any wilting or dirty leaves. Brussels sprouts vary in size. If yours are smaller, keep them whole; otherwise halve or quarter them. Combine the vegetables, olive oil, rosemary, thyme and pinch of salt in a large bowl. Spread the vegetables in a large rimmed baking pan and roast them in the oven for 15 to 20 minutes, stirring halfway, until they are lightly browned.

While the vegetables are roasting, cook the bulgur. Check the packaging on how to cook the bulgur, as it can come in many different sizes. Usually bulgur is cooked by pouring twice the amount of boiling water (1 cup [240 ml] of boiling water for ½ cup [70 g] of bulgur) over the bulgur in a bowl. Cover the bowl and let it stand for 20 to 30 minutes until the water has been absorbed. Fluff the bulgur with a fork.

Once the vegetables are done roasting, remove them from the oven and add them to a large pot. Add vegetable broth and bring the soup to a boil over medium-high heat. Once it is boiling, reduce the heat and simmer for 5 minutes until all the vegetables are tender. Stir the cooked bulgur into the soup and add the balsamic vinegar. Season the soup with salt and pepper to taste.

PER 1 CUP (240 ML) SERVING WITHOUT GARNISHES: CALORIES 155 ⇉ FAT 4 G ⇉ CARBOHYDRATES 23.4 G ⇉ FIBER 7.2 G ⇉ PROTEIN 8.7 G

BROCCOLI "CHEDDAR" SOUP

MAKES 1 QUART (950 ML)

I hate to admit it but every once in a while I get envious of people ordering a bowl of broccoli cheddar soup. Instead of ordering it myself, I wanted to make a vegan version that would taste better and be far healthier. Once you've made the vegan cheddar cheese sauce recipe, making this broccoli cheddar soup is a breeze.

2 tsp (10 ml) olive oil

1 yellow onion, diced

4 cups (280 g) broccoli florets

1 cup (200 g) Vegan Cheddar Cheese Sauce (page 186)

2 cups (480 ml) water

2 cups (480 ml) vegetable broth

Salt and pepper

Heat the olive oil in a pot and add the onion. Cook the onion over medium-high heat for 5 minutes until it starts to become translucent. Reduce the heat and add the broccoli and cheese sauce. Stir to coat the broccoli with cheese sauce before adding the water and vegetable broth. Bring all the ingredients to a boil, then reduce the heat, cover and simmer for 15 to 20 minutes until the broccoli is cooked.

Purée the soup using an immersion blender or in batches in a blender. Season the soup with salt and pepper to taste before serving.

PER 1 CUP (240 ML) SERVING: CALORIES 198 ⫸ FAT 12.6 G ⫸ CARBOHYDRATES 16.9 G ⫸ FIBER 5.6 G ⫸ PROTEIN 7.5 G

CREAMY POTATO BEET SOUP WITH HORSERADISH

MAKES 2 QUARTS (1.9 L)

Horseradish can easily become overpowering, but when added correctly, it can give your food just the right amount of zing. Horseradish is generally not cooked. So it may seem weird to wait to stir it into the soup at the very end, but it also allows you to add just the right amount to your taste.

2 beetroots (around 200 g each or 400 g together)

1 lb (455 g) potatoes

1 tbsp (15 ml) olive oil

1 small yellow onion, diced

2 cloves garlic, minced

½ tsp fresh or dried rosemary

½ tsp fresh or dried thyme

4 cups (960 ml) vegetable broth

1 cup (240 ml) almond milk or other plant-based milk

1 tsp or more grated, fresh horseradish, optional

Fresh parsley, for garnish

Homemade Croutons (page 184), for garnish

Peel and dice the beetroot and potatoes and set them aside.

Heat the olive oil in a pot over medium-high heat and add the diced onion. Cook the onion for 5 to 7 minutes. Add the minced garlic, rosemary and thyme to the pot and cook for another 3 to 4 minutes until the garlic and herbs become fragrant. Put the diced potatoes and beetroot in the pot and cook for another 4 minutes, stirring frequently. Add the vegetable broth and milk and bring the soup to a boil. Once the soup is boiling, reduce the heat and allow it to simmer for 25 to 40 minutes until the beets and potatoes are tender.

Remove from the heat and purée the soup using an immersion blender, or in batches in a blender, until smooth. Stir in the grated horseradish and serve the soup hot with some fresh parsley and homemade croutons.

PER 1 CUP (240 ML) SERVING WITHOUT GARNISHES: CALORIES 170 ⋙ FAT 9.8 G ⋙ CARBOHYDRATES 17.3 G ⋙ FIBER 3.3 G ⋙ PROTEIN 5.1 G

INDIAN LENTIL SOUP WITH KALE AND CILANTRO

MAKES 1½ QUARTS (1.4 L)

More lentils! Some people hate them and others love them. However, lentils play such a vital role in a whole food, plant-based diet. Not only are they rich in fiber, but are also a great and much-needed sources of plant-based iron.

1 cup (240 ml) vegetable broth

1 cup (240 ml) water

1 cup (200 g) yellow lentils

1 onion

2 tsp (10 ml) coconut oil

2 cloves garlic, minced

2 tsp (4 g) grated, fresh ginger

¼ tsp mustard seeds

½ tsp ground coriander

2 tsp (4 g) garam masala

1 tsp ground fenugreek

1 tsp ground cumin

1 tsp ground turmeric

½ tsp or more ground cayenne pepper, optional

2 cups (480 ml) tomato purée

1 cup (20 g) finely chopped kale

½ cup (12 g) chopped cilantro, leaves and stems, plus more for garnish

Salt

Whole grain bread, for serving

Add the vegetable broth, water and lentils to a saucepan and bring it to a boil. Once boiling, reduce the heat and allow the lentils to simmer for 15 minutes until they are tender.

While the lentils are cooking, dice the onion. Heat the coconut oil in a pot and add the onions. Cook the onions for 5 minutes until they begin to become translucent. Add the garlic, ginger and spices and cook for 1 to 2 minutes until the spices and garlic become fragrant. Add the tomato purée to the pot.

Once the lentils are cooked, add them, along with the water and broth they cooked in, to the pot. Simmer the soup while you remove the thick stems and finely chop the kale. Chop the cilantro now as well before stirring it along with the kale in the pot.

Season the soup with salt to taste and garnish with more fresh cilantro. Serve the soup with a piece of whole grain bread.

PER 1 CUP (240 ML) SERVING WITHOUT GARNISHES: CALORIES 226 ⋙ FAT 13 G ⋙ CARBOHYDRATES 23 G ⋙ FIBER 4.4 G ⋙ PROTEIN 8.6 G

CREAMY ALMOND SOUP

MAKES 2 QUARTS (1.9 L)

This soup is my love declaration to almonds. Raw almonds are my go-to snack, almond butter is my favorite spread and almond milk has been adding delicious creaminess to my coffee for the past four years. So it was obvious to me that if I was going to make an almond soup that I would add all three.

1 small yellow onion

2 cloves garlic

1 small head (roughly 270 g) cauliflower

1 tsp olive oil

4 cups (960 ml) vegetable broth, divided

2 tbsp (30 g) almond butter

2 cups (350 g) cannellini beans, soaked and cooked or rinsed and drained from a can

2 cups (480 ml) almond milk

¼ cup (23 g) sliced almonds, for garnish

Salt and pepper

Parsley, for garnish

Dice the onion, mince the garlic and chop the cauliflower into florets. Heat the olive oil in a pot over medium-high heat and add the diced onion. Cook the onion for 5 to 7 minutes until it begins to become translucent. Add the garlic and cauliflower florets and cook for 4 to 5 minutes until the garlic becomes fragrant.

Add 3 cups (720 ml) of vegetable broth to the pot. Whisk the remaining cup (240 ml) of broth with the almond butter to make a paste before adding it to the pot along with the beans. Cook for 10 minutes until the cauliflower is tender.

Purée the soup using an immersion blender or in batches in a blender. Return the soup to the pot and add the almond milk. Bring the soup to another boil. Once the soup is boiling, reduce the heat and simmer for 5 minutes.

While the soup is cooking, dry roast the sliced almonds in a pan over medium-high heat, stirring constantly until the almonds are lightly browned. The almonds will burn very easily, so watch them carefully.

Season the soup with more salt and pepper to taste. Serve the soup with sliced almonds and parsley.

PER 1 CUP (240 ML) SERVING WITHOUT GARNISHES: CALORIES 328 ⇒⇒⇒ FAT 16.7 G ⇒⇒⇒ CARBOHYDRATES 33.1 G ⇒⇒⇒ FIBER 13.4 G ⇒⇒⇒ PROTEIN 15.2 G

CURRIED CHICKPEA KALE SOUP

MAKES 1½ QUARTS (1.4 L)

Low on protein? This is your vegan protein fix. What's even better is that it will take you less than fifteen minutes to make it.

1 tbsp (15 ml) olive oil

1 small yellow onion, diced

2 tbsp (12 g) yellow curry powder

2 cloves garlic, minced

3 cups (500 g) cooked chickpeas, soaked and cooked or rinsed and drained from a can

2 cups (480 ml) tomato purée

3 cups (720 ml) water

4 oz (113 g) kale

Salt and pepper

Heat the olive oil in a pot over medium-high heat. Add the onion and cook for 5 minutes until it begins to brown, then stir in the curry powder and garlic. Cook for 2 more minutes until the curry powder and garlic become fragrant. Add the chickpeas, tomato purée and water. Bring these to a boil, then reduce the heat and simmer.

Rinse the kale under cold water, remove the woody stems and chop the leaves. Lay the chopped kale leaves on top of the soup and allow the steam from the soup to cook the kale. After 5 to 10 minutes of simmering, season the soup with salt and pepper to taste before serving.

PER 1 CUP (240 ML) SERVING WITHOUT GARNISHES: CALORIES 377 ⇒⇒⇒ FAT 7.8 G ⇒⇒⇒ CARBOHYDRATES 62.6 G ⇒⇒⇒ FIBER 17.3 G ⇒⇒⇒ PROTEIN 18.5 G

WINTER DETOX SOUP

MAKES 2 QUARTS (1.9 L)

I always find this soup is perfect after the holidays when I've indulged in too many rich and heavy foods. I like to swap my usual dinner for a bowl of this soup instead.

Doing a weeklong detox during the winter isn't the best idea. However, this winter detox soup can give your digestive system a quick break. It doesn't contain oils, salt or grains, making it very easy to digest. A salt-less soup can take some getting used to. If you really need it, add a bit of salt.

6 cups (1.4 L) water

2 cloves garlic, minced

1 tsp grated, fresh ginger

1 red onion, diced

½ small red cabbage (8 oz [226 g]), chopped

1 carrot, diced

1 rib celery, diced

1 small head broccoli (cut into florets, it should equal roughly 2 cups [120 g])

4 radishes, chopped

2 cups (30 g) chopped kale

1 tsp grated, fresh turmeric (alternatively use ¼ tsp dried turmeric)

2 cardamom pods, seeds ground (alternatively use ⅛ tsp dried cardamom)

½ tsp cayenne pepper, optional

½ cup (20 g) fresh parsley, chopped

Fresh lemon juice

Heat the water in a large pot over high heat. Add all of the ingredients except for the lemon juice. I like my vegetables to have a nice crunch to them in this soup, so I cook them for only about 5 minutes. If you want your vegetables to be more tender, increase the cook time anywhere from 10 to 30 minutes. If you cook your vegetables longer, you may need to add more water while cooking.

Remove the pot from the heat and add as much lemon juice as you like before serving.

PER 1 CUP (240 ML) SERVING WITHOUT GARNISHES: CALORIES 27 ⋙ FAT 0.2 G ⋙ CARBOHYDRATES 5.9 G ⋙ FIBER 1.9 G ⋙ PROTEIN 1.3 G

CREAMY BRUSSELS SPROUT SOUP

MAKES 2 QUARTS (1.9 L)

Most people don't like Brussels sprouts. I used to despise them because I associated them with overcooked, under-seasoned, smelly lumps of greenery around Christmas time. That was before I realized that you can make them taste great.

This soup is a perfect way to ease back into the Brussels sprout taste without being overwhelmed by it. Plus, it's always enjoyable telling friends and family that they just slurped down a soup that contained probably more Brussels sprouts than they have eaten in the past ten years.

1 lb (453 g) Brussels sprouts

1 tbsp (15 ml) olive oil

3 shallots, diced

3 cloves garlic

1 carrot, diced

1 red bell pepper, diced

2 tbsp (4 g) chopped, fresh parsley or
1 tsp dried parsley, plus more for garnish

3 cups (720 ml) vegetable broth

2 cups (480 ml) plant-based milk

Salt and pepper

Hot sauce, optional

Rinse off the Brussels sprouts with cold water to remove any dirt. Then, use a small knife to cut off the tip of the stem of each Brussels sprout and toss it. If any of the outer leaves of the Brussels sprouts have blemishes or dirt that can't be removed, take those leaves off and throw them away. Chop the Brussels sprouts and set them in a bowl for later use.

Heat the olive oil over medium-high heat in a pot and add the shallots, garlic, carrot, bell pepper and Brussels sprouts. If you are using fresh parsley, set a tablespoon (2 g) of it aside for garnish before adding the rest of it to the pot. Cook, stirring occasionally, for roughly 5 minutes until the garlic becomes fragrant and the Brussels sprouts start to brown. Add the broth and milk to the pot and bring the soup to a boil. Once it is boiling, reduce the heat and simmer for 20 minutes. Purée the soup using an immersion blender, or in batches in a blender, until smooth.

Season the soup with salt and pepper if needed. This soup tastes great with a few drops of hot sauce and fresh parsley.

PER 1 CUP (240 ML) SERVING WITHOUT GARNISHES: CALORIES 74 ⇒ FAT 2.8 G ⇒ CARBOHYDRATES 9.4 G ⇒ FIBER 2.6 G ⇒ PROTEIN 4.3 G

ROASTED ROOT VEGETABLE SOUP

MAKES 2 QUARTS (1.9 L)

Winter is all about root vegetables. Some of them may be really ugly (looking at you, celeriac!)
but they deserve to be showcased.

2 cups (270 g) diced rutabaga

½ lb (226 g) potatoes, diced

1 cup (120 g) diced parsnips

1 cup (120 g) diced large carrot

2 cups (150 g) diced celeriac

1 tbsp (15 ml) olive oil

2 cups (480 ml) vegetable broth

4 cups (960 ml) water

2 cloves garlic, minced

1 bay leaf

2 thyme sprigs

Salt and pepper

Preheat the oven to 425°F (220°C) and line a baking tray with parchment paper.

Peel and dice the rutabaga, potatoes, parsnips, carrot and celeriac. Coat the vegetables with the olive oil and spread them on the lined baking tray. Roast them in the oven for 40 minutes, turning them halfway through. Keep a close eye on the vegetables. The cook time will vary slightly depending on the size of your diced vegetables.

While the vegetables are cooking, heat the broth and water in a large pot over medium heat. Add the minced garlic, bay leaf and thyme to the pot and let it slowly simmer.

Once the vegetables are tender, add them to the pot, cook for 2 minutes, and season with salt and pepper to taste. Remove the bay leaf and thyme sprigs before serving.

PER 1 CUP (240 ML) SERVING WITHOUT GARNISHES: CALORIES 87 »»»» FAT 2.3 G
»»»» CARBOHYDRATES 14.6 G »»»» FIBER 3.2 G »»»» PROTEIN 2.9 G

CREAMY RUTABAGA SOUP

MAKES 1 QUART (950 ML)

Rutabaga can seem very intimidating when you first encounter it. The easiest way to approach it is by cutting off the ends first and then slicing vertically down the middle. Now, I like to treat my rutabaga like a cantaloupe. Cut it into slices and use a good paring knife to cut off the tough skin. That's much easier than trying to use a potato peeler. The delicious, peppery taste of the rutabaga is well worth the knife work.

2 cups (270 g) diced and peeled rutabaga

½ lb (226 g) potatoes, diced and peeled

2 tsp (10 ml) olive oil, plus more for cooking

1 yellow onion, diced

2 cloves garlic, minced

1 rib celery, diced

½ tsp dried thyme

¼ tsp dried rosemary

2 cups (480 ml) vegetable broth

1 cup (240 ml) unsweetened almond milk

Salt

Fresh, chopped parsley, for garnish

Preheat the oven to 425°F (220°C) and line a baking tray with parchment paper.

Coat the rutabaga and potatoes with the olive oil and spread on the lined baking tray. Roast them in the oven for 40 minutes, turning them halfway through. Watch the vegetables closely. It may take less or more time to roast them depending on the dice of the vegetables.

With roughly 20 minutes left for your rutabaga and potatoes to cook, heat more olive oil in a pot over medium-high heat. Add the onion and cook for 5 to 7 minutes until it becomes translucent. Add the garlic, celery, thyme and rosemary and cook for 2 minutes before adding the broth and almond milk. Reduce the heat and let the soup simmer.

Once the rutabaga and potatoes are tender, add them to the pot, reserving about ¼ of them. Use an immersion blender to purée the soup until smooth, or blend in batches in a blender. Season the soup with salt to taste. Serve the soup and garnish it with the reserved roasted vegetables and some fresh, chopped parsley.

PER 1 CUP (240 ML) SERVING WITHOUT GARNISHES: CALORIES 127 ⇶ FAT 4.2 G ⇶ CARBOHYDRATES 18.7 G ⇶ FIBER 4.1 G ⇶ PROTEIN 4.9 G

COCONUT GARLIC BEET SOUP

MAKES 1 QUART (950 ML)

Beets might not be everyone's favorite, but there is no denying they make for a pretty colored soup. Make sure to add the lemon juice to this soup. It gives the soup a nice acidity that balances out the sweetness from the beets.

2 beetroots (around 200 g each, or 400 g together)

1 tbsp (15 ml) olive oil

2 cloves garlic, minced

¼ cup (15 g) chopped parsley, plus more for garnish

2 cups (480 ml) vegetable broth

1 to 2 tsp (5 to 10 ml) fresh lemon juice

1 (13.5-oz [400-ml]) can coconut milk, plus more for garnish

Salt and pepper

Lemon slices, for garnish

Peel and dice the beetroots and set aside.

Heat the olive oil in a pot over medium-high heat and cook the garlic for 2 minutes until it becomes fragrant. Add the parsley and diced beets to the pot and cook for an additional 2 minutes. Add the vegetable broth and bring it to a boil. Once boiling, reduce the heat and allow the soup to simmer for 20 minutes until the beets are tender. Add 1 teaspoon of lemon juice and the can of coconut milk to the soup and cook for 5 more minutes.

Then, purée the soup using an immersion blender or in batches in a blender. Season the soup with salt and pepper to taste and add more lemon juice if desired. Serve the soup hot in bowls and garnish with more coconut milk, parsley and lemon.

PER 1 CUP (240 ML) SERVING WITHOUT GARNISHES: CALORIES 331 ⋙
FAT 28.6 G ⋙ CARBOHYDRATES 16.8 G ⋙ FIBER 4.4 G ⋙ PROTEIN 6.7 G

RED CABBAGE POTATO SOUP

MAKES 3 QUARTS (2.8 L)

I never grow tired of looking at the gorgeous purple hue that comes from red cabbage. Making a red cabbage soup is a nice change from the all too often seen braised and pickled red cabbage, plus it tastes way better!

1 small red cabbage (roughly 1.8 lb [815 g])

1 lb (455 g) potatoes

1 tbsp (15 ml) olive oil

1 small yellow onion

2 cloves garlic, minced

8 cups (1.9 L) vegetable broth

½ tsp or more fresh lemon juice

Salt and pepper

Homemade Croutons (page 184), for garnish

Vegan Sour Cream (page 180), for garnish

Peel off the outer leaves of the red cabbage and discard them. Cut the cabbage in half or quarter it and remove the tough stem. Chop the red cabbage and peel and dice the potatoes.

Heat the olive oil in a large stock pot over medium-high heat. Dice the yellow onion and add it to the pot. Cook the onion for 5 minutes until it begins to become translucent. Add the minced garlic, cabbage and potatoes. Allow them to cook for 5 minutes, stirring often. Add the vegetable broth and bring the soup to a boil. Once boiling, reduce the heat, cover the pot and allow the soup to simmer for at least 20 minutes, until the cabbage and potatoes are tender.

Purée the soup using an immersion blender or in batches in a blender. Add the lemon juice to the soup, starting with ½ teaspoon and adding more to taste.

Season the soup with salt and pepper to taste. Serve soup hot with homemade croutons and a dollop of vegan sour cream.

PER 1 CUP (240 ML) SERVING WITHOUT GARNISHES: CALORIES 79 ⇒⇒⇒ FAT 2.2 G ⇒⇒⇒ CARBOHYDRATES 10.6 G ⇒⇒⇒ FIBER 2.5 G ⇒⇒⇒ PROTEIN 4.7 G

INDIAN BEETROOT STEW

MAKES 2 QUARTS (1.9 L)

Indian spices pair incredibly well with beetroots. It elevates this stew into something that I crave over and over again.
Try it with some healthy brown rice for a complete and filling meal!

2 beetroots (around 200 g each or 400 g together)

1 lb (455 g) potatoes

1⅓ cups (240 g) diced tomatoes

1 tbsp (15 ml) coconut oil

1 small yellow onion, diced

2 cloves garlic, minced

1 tsp fresh grated ginger

¼ tsp turmeric

½ tsp ground coriander

1 tsp garam masala

2 cups (480 ml) of water

1 bay leaf

Salt

Cilantro, for garnish

Grated coconut, for garnish

Peel and dice the beets and potatoes and finely dice the tomatoes. Set the beets, potatoes and tomatoes aside for later use.

Heat the coconut oil in a pot over medium-high heat and add the onion. Cook for 7 to 9 minutes until the onion begins to brown. Add the garlic, ginger, turmeric, coriander, garam masala, beets, potatoes and tomatoes to the pot and cook, stirring often, for at least 5 minutes until the spices become fragrant. Add the water and bay leaf and bring it to a boil. Cover the pot, reduce the heat and allow the stew to simmer for 20 minutes.

If the stew is not thick enough, uncover and continue to cook it until it thickens to your liking. Remove the bay leaf and season the stew with salt to taste and serve hot. Garnish with fresh cilantro and grated coconut.

PER 1 CUP (240 ML) SERVING WITHOUT GARNISHES: CALORIES 89 ⫸ FAT 2.0 G ⫸ CARBOHYDRATES 16.9 G ⫸ FIBER 3.1 G ⫸ PROTEIN 2.4 G

CREAMY PARSNIP PEAR SOUP

MAKES 1 QUART (950 ML)

This recipe came about as an accident. I originally wanted to make a parsnip apple soup.
However, I didn't have any apples left and only pears at home. I was skeptical at first but the combination
of parsnips and pears works beautifully together. Don't forget the balsamic reduction sauce!

1 tbsp (15 ml) olive oil

1 small yellow onion, diced

2 cloves garlic, minced

1 tsp dried or fresh thyme

1¼ lb (570 g) parsnips, peeled and diced

2 pears, peeled and diced

3 cups (720 ml) vegetable broth

Balsamic reduction or vinegar, for garnish

Fresh chopped parsley, for garnish

Heat the olive oil in a pot over medium-high heat and add the onion. Cook the onion for roughly 7 minutes before adding the garlic, thyme, parsnips and pears. Cook for 5 minutes, stirring occasionally and being careful not to let the garlic brown. Add the vegetable broth and bring the soup to a boil. Once boiling, reduce the heat and allow the soup to simmer for 20 minutes until the parsnips are tender.

Purée the soup using an immersion blender, or in batches in a blender, until smooth. Serve the soup hot with a balsamic reduction drizzle and fresh chopped parsley.

PER 1 CUP (240 ML) SERVING WITHOUT GARNISHES: CALORIES 236 ⇛ FAT 5.2 G ⇛ CARBOHYDRATES 44.5 G ⇛ FIBER 10.7 G ⇛ PROTEIN 6.0 G

BLACK BEAN SOUP

MAKES 1 QUART (950 ML)

Beans, beans, beans—the magical source of plant-based protein, folate and fiber.
Be sure to load up this healthy black bean soup with all your favorite fixins.

1 cup (200 g) dried black beans (alternatively use 2 [15-oz (425-g)] cans black beans, rinsed and drained—see note)

2 cups (480 ml) vegetable broth

2 cups (480 ml) water

1 small yellow onion, finely diced

3 cloves garlic, minced

1 rib celery, finely diced

1 large carrot, finely diced

2 tsp (5 g) cumin

1 tbsp (7 g) paprika

1 tsp cayenne pepper, optional

1 cup (240 ml) tomato purée

Salt

Vegan Sour Cream (page 180), for garnish

Fresh chopped cilantro, for garnish

½ avocado, diced, for garnish

Soak your dried beans in cold water overnight.

Rinse the beans the next day and place them in a pot with the vegetable broth and water. Bring it to a boil over high heat then reduce the heat, cover and simmer for an hour. If a lot of foam builds up, just use a spoon to skim it off.

After the beans have simmered for an hour, add the onion, garlic, celery and carrot. Continue to simmer the soup, covered, for 30 minutes. Then add the cumin, paprika, cayenne pepper and tomato purée and simmer again, covered, for 30 minutes. The beans should now be cooked.

I like using an immersion blender to slightly purée the soup while still leaving it a bit chunky. This is completely optional. You can leave the beans whole or purée them completely.

If the soup is too thin for your liking, let it simmer, uncovered, until the desired thickness is achieved.

Season the soup with salt to taste before serving with a dollop of vegan sour cream, cilantro and diced avocado.

PER 1 CUP (240 ML) SERVING WITHOUT GARNISHES: CALORIES 264 ⫸⫸ FAT 2.2 G ⫸⫸ CARBOHYDRATES 47.1 G ⫸⫸ FIBER 11.6 G ⫸⫸ PROTEIN 16.6 G

NOTE

⫸⫸ This soup can be made using canned black beans if needed. I do have to point out though that it tastes far better using dried black beans. If you are using canned beans, add all the ingredients, minus 1 cup (240 ml) of water, to the pot and simmer for 30 minutes uncovered before puréeing it and serving it with vegan sour cream, cilantro and avocado.

COCONUT BOK CHOY SOUP WITH VERMICELLI

MAKES 1 QUART (950 ML)

Bok choy is easily found in the winter, but it is usually added to dishes as a side note. I wanted this easy soup to really highlight the bok choy, without it being overwhelming. It's a fairly light soup that I like making as a quick lunch. My kids love slurping the vermicelli. If you omit or wait until the end to add the red Thai pepper to your soup, it's actually quite mild and kid-friendly.

8 oz (226 g) baby bok choy

1 tsp coconut oil

1 tsp grated, fresh ginger

2 cloves garlic, minced

½ tsp lemon zest

½ tsp lime zest

1 tsp grated, fresh turmeric (alternatively use ¼ tsp dried turmeric)

1 red Thai pepper, chopped, plus more, sliced, for garnish

¼ cup (60 ml) lime juice

¼ cup (60 ml) water

1 (13.5-oz [400-ml]) can coconut milk

¼ tsp salt

2 oz (57 g) mung bean vermicelli

Bean sprouts, for garnish

Cilantro, for garnish

Cut off the root ends of the bok choy, remove the leaves and chop them. Set them aside.

In a large pan, heat the coconut oil over medium-high heat and add the ginger, garlic, lemon zest, lime zest, turmeric and red Thai pepper. Cook for 2 minutes before adding the lime juice and chopped bok choy, then cook for another 2 minutes. Add the water, coconut milk and salt and let it simmer for 5 minutes. Season the soup with more salt to taste.

Meanwhile, in a separate bowl, pour boiling water over the vermicelli and let it sit for 5 minutes or until the noodles are cooked. Drain the water from the noodles. Divide the noodles between 2 or 4 bowls and pour the coconut bok choy soup over the noodles. Garnish with bean sprouts, fresh cilantro and sliced red Thai pepper. Serve immediately.

PER 1 CUP (240 ML) SERVING WITHOUT GARNISHES: CALORIES 276 ≫≫ FAT 25.7 G ≫≫ CARBOHYDRATES 12.1 G ≫≫ FIBER 3.3 G ≫≫ PROTEIN 3.6 G

CREAM OF ENDIVE SOUP

MAKES 1 QUART (950 ML)

Endive is another winter vegetable many people don't use. I was put off by its bitter taste at first.
Once you cook it, the bitterness subsides slightly and it actually has a slight sweet note to it.

2 tsp (10 ml) coconut oil

1 yellow onion, diced

2 (300 g) endives, chopped coarsely

1 (300 g) potato, peeled and diced

3 cloves garlic, minced

1 cup (240 ml) vegetable broth

1 cup (240 ml) water

1 cup (240 ml) unsweetened almond milk

2 tsp (10 ml) fresh lemon juice

Salt and pepper

¼ cup (40 g) raw almonds, for garnish

¼ cup (43 g) raw hazelnuts, for garnish

Chopped fresh parsley, for garnish

½ cup (80 g) pomegranate seeds, for garnish

Heat the coconut oil in a pot over medium heat. Add the onion and chopped endives to the pot and cook for 5 to 7 minutes. The endive will begin to wilt and the onion will become translucent. Then, add the diced potatoes and garlic. Cook for another 10 minutes, stirring occasionally.

Add the vegetable broth, water and almond milk and let the soup simmer for another 10 minutes. Check to make sure the potatoes are tender before puréeing it with an immersion blender. Alternatively, you can blend the soup in a blender in batches.

Stir the lemon juice into the soup and season with salt and pepper to taste.

Roughly chop the almonds and hazelnuts before serving them over the soup with some chopped parsley and pomegranate seeds.

PER 1 CUP (240 ML) SERVING WITHOUT GARNISHES: CALORIES 244 ⋙ FAT 13.3 G ⋙ CARBOHYDRATES 26.5 G ⋙ FIBER 7.0 G ⋙ PROTEIN 7.8 G

RUTABAGA, SQUASH AND PASTA SOUP

MAKES 2 QUARTS (1.9 L)

Sometimes you just need a good soup with some pasta to fill and warm you up. The squash and rutabaga are just an added seasonal, vitamin boost that we could all use.

4 cups (960 ml) vegetable broth

4 cups (960 ml) water

1 sprig fresh rosemary

1 yellow onion, diced

2 cups (260 g) diced squash

2 cups (270 g) diced rutabaga

2 cups (230 g) whole grain pasta

2 cloves garlic, minced

Salt and pepper

Heat the vegetable broth, water and rosemary in a large pot over medium-high heat. Add the onion, squash and rutabaga and cook for 5 minutes. The squash and rutabaga should be almost tender at this point.

Add the pasta and garlic to the pot. Cook until the noodles are tender. The cook time will vary depending on the type of pasta you use.

Remove the sprig of rosemary from the pot. Season the soup with salt and pepper to taste before serving.

PER 1 CUP (240 ML) SERVING WITHOUT GARNISHES: CALORIES 110 ⋙ FAT 1.3 G ⋙ CARBOHYDRATES 19.6 G ⋙ FIBER 3.5 G ⋙ PROTEIN 5.8 G

BROCCOLI POTATO CHOWDER

MAKES 2 QUARTS (1.9 L)

A chowder with broccoli and potatoes is a nice alternative to a corn chowder. It's creamy yet light with a slight cheesy flavor, thanks to the nutritional yeast. Don't forget the diced red bell peppers on top. They add a crisp crunch that's much healthier than crackers.

6 cups (1.4 L) vegetable broth

1 yellow onion, diced

8 oz (227 g) broccoli florets

1 lb (454 g) potatoes, peeled and diced

1 tsp chopped fresh thyme or ½ tsp dried thyme

2 tbsp (11 g) chickpea flour

2 cups (480 ml) unsweetened almond milk

¼ cup (10 g) nutritional yeast

Salt and pepper

1 red bell pepper, finely diced, for garnish

Add the broth, onion, broccoli, potatoes and thyme in a large pot. Bring the broth to a boil, then reduce the heat, cover and simmer for 15 minutes until the potatoes are tender.

In a bowl, whisk the chickpea flour, almond milk and nutritional yeast together. Slowly add the mixture to the soup. Cook the chowder for another 5 minutes, stirring often.

Season the chowder with salt and pepper to taste. Ladle the chowder into bowls and garnish with some diced bell pepper.

PER 1 CUP (240 ML) SERVING WITHOUT GARNISHES: CALORIES 122 ⟫⟫⟩ FAT 2.5 G ⟫⟫⟩ CARBOHYDRATES 17.5 G ⟫⟫⟩ FIBER 4.5 G ⟫⟫⟩ PROTEIN 8.7 G

BRIGHT AND FRAGRANT SPRING SOUPS

With the first signs of spring, we no longer want rich, comforting soups. Instead we want soups that give us a sense of lightness with crisp, fresh flavors. As much as we would like, the beginning of spring doesn't offer us a boundless amount of produce. However, there is a wonderful selection of green produce available. Baby spinach, artichoke, asparagus and peas are some of my favorites.

The increase in sunlight makes springtime ideal for growing your own herbs. If you cook with herbs the way I do, then plant way more herbs than you think you might need because you WILL need them. The Fresh Herb Soup (page 120) with homegrown herbs will taste terrific!

In come these beautiful broth-based spring vegetable soups. Nearly all of the flavor is packed in just the broths. Let's just say if I were a vegetable I would want to swim in these broths. They are much simpler than they look, and they taste like a parade in your mouth!

WHAT'S IN SEASON
ARTICHOKE – ASPARAGUS – BROCCOLI – FENNEL – LEEKS –
PEAS – SPINACH

EASY ARTICHOKE SOUP

MAKES 1 QUART (950 ML)

The very first time I bought an artichoke was solely for the reason that I thought it looked cool. I had no idea how to cut it. I was also utterly confused by how completely different canned and fresh artichokes looked. After I completely butchered the artichoke, I gave it another try a week later. I realized that canned artichokes should only be used in an emergency and that fresh artichokes were what was missing in my life all along.

What makes this artichoke soup easy is that you don't have to cook the artichoke separately.
All the veggies get cooked together at once.

2 artichokes (or six artichoke hearts if you are using canned artichokes)

1 rib celery, diced

1 leek, white and light green parts only, sliced

2 cloves garlic, chopped

1 yellow onion, diced

1 tbsp (15 ml) olive oil

5 cups (1.2 L) vegetable broth

1 bay leaf

1 cup (40 g) fresh parsley

Homemade Croutons (page 184)

Salt

Using a serrated knife, cut the top third of the artichoke off and throw it away. Cut off the stem, remove ½ inch (1.3 cm) off the bottom and use a peeler to peel away the thick outer layer. Dice the stem and add to a pot. Using a paring knife, cut off the thick leaves of the artichoke. Cut the artichoke in half and remove the choke with a spoon. The choke is the hairy, fuzzy part in the middle that you want to throw away. What you are left with now is the artichoke heart. Add this to the pot as well and repeat the steps above with the second artichoke.

Add the diced celery, leek, garlic, onion and olive oil to the pot as well. Cook the vegetables for 5 minutes on medium-high heat. Artichoke oxidizes very quickly and will turn brown. This is completely normal.

After letting the vegetables cook, add the vegetable broth, bay leaf and parsley. Bring the broth to a boil, reduce the heat, cover and simmer for 30 minutes. While the soup is simmering, prepare the croutons.

Remove the bay leaf from the pot before puréeing the soup with an immersion blender or in batches in a blender. Season the soup with salt to taste before serving with the homemade croutons.

PER 1 CUP (240 ML) SERVING WITHOUT GARNISHES: CALORIES 149 FAT 5.6 G CARBOHYDRATES 16.9 G FIBER 6.0 G PROTEIN 9.9 G

LEMON ASPARAGUS SOUP

MAKES 1 QUART (950 ML)

I get really excited when asparagus is in season. I buy so much of it that I always have a large pile of asparagus sitting on my kitchen counter ready to be used. My kids call it the "asparagus mountain." There are so many healthy asparagus recipes but one of my favorites is this lemon asparagus soup. It's simple, healthy and tastes bright and light. Perfect for spring!

12 asparagus spears

1 medium yellow onion, diced

4 cups (960 ml) low-sodium vegetable broth, divided

3 cloves garlic, minced

1 tbsp (15 ml) fresh lemon juice

1 cup (240 ml) unsweetened almond milk

Snap off the woody root end of each asparagus spear at its natural breaking point, or cut off roughly 2 inches (5 cm) and discard. Steam the asparagus in a steamer for 5 to 7 minutes until tender. If you don't have a steamer, bring a large stockpot filled with water and 1 teaspoon of salt to a boil. Cook the asparagus for 3 to 5 minutes until bright green and tender. Remove the asparagus from the steamer or pot and rinse under cold water. Cut off the tips of 8 of the asparagus stalks and set aside.

Add the diced onion and 2 cups (473 ml) of the vegetable broth to a large stockpot, over high heat. Once boiling, reduce to low-medium heat and simmer for 10 minutes until the onion softens.

Add the garlic and steamed asparagus (don't add the tips that were cut off) to the stockpot and allow to simmer for 2 more minutes.

Mix the lemon juice and remaining vegetable broth into the stockpot and purée the soup using an immersion blender or in batches in a blender. Return the puréed soup to pot and add the almond milk. Bring the soup to a quick boil over medium-high heat. Once boiling, reduce to low-medium heat and simmer for 15 minutes, stirring occasionally, until the soup thickens. Add the asparagus tips to the soup and cook for 1 more minute.

Pour the soup into bowls, making sure that each bowl has a couple asparagus tips.

PER 1 CUP (240 ML) SERVING WITHOUT GARNISHES: CALORIES 55 FAT 1.0 G CARBOHYDRATES 10.7 G FIBER 2.4 G PROTEIN 2.3 G

CREAMY LEEK SOUP WITH WILD RICE

MAKES 2 QUARTS (1.9 L)

Leeks are available from autumn until spring. Though this soup could be made at any time, it's one I like to make in early spring. Rainy spring days really call for a bowl of creamy soup to cheer you up!

2 leeks

1 tbsp (15 ml) olive oil

3 cloves garlic, minced

1 lb (453 g) potatoes, peeled and diced

1 tbsp (2 g) fresh rosemary, finely chopped

½ tsp fresh thyme

4 cups (960 ml) vegetable broth

1 cup (240 ml) water

2 cups (480 ml) plant-based milk

1 cup (170 g) uncooked wild rice

Salt and pepper

Bread, for serving

Cut off the dark green leaves from your leeks. You can either throw these leaves away or keep them for later to make a broth. Chop the white part of the leeks into thin rings. The sliced leeks should weigh roughly 12 ounces (340 g). Place the sliced leeks in a bowl of cold water. Rinse them thoroughly to remove any dirt. Drain the water from the bowl and set the leeks aside.

Heat the olive oil in a large pot and add the minced garlic, leeks, potatoes, rosemary and thyme. Cook everything in the pot over medium heat for 5 to 7 minutes, until the garlic becomes fragrant and the leeks become slightly limp. Add the vegetable broth and water and bring to a boil. Once the soup is boiling, reduce the heat and simmer for 20 minutes until the leeks and potatoes are tender.

Purée the soup with an immersion blender, or in a blender in batches, until smooth. Add the milk and rice to the soup and bring to another boil. Reduce the heat and simmer, stirring often to prevent the rice from sticking to the bottom of the pot, for 20 to 30 minutes until the rice is tender.

Season the soup with salt and pepper to taste. Serve the soup with a slice of bread, if you like.

PER 1 CUP (240 ML) SERVING WITHOUT GARNISHES: CALORIES 178 ⫸⫸ FAT 3.5 G ⫸⫸ CARBOHYDRATES 29.9 G ⫸⫸ FIBER 3.4 G ⫸⫸ PROTEIN 7.9 G

ROASTED FENNEL POTATO SOUP

MAKES 1 QUART (950 ML)

Fennel wasn't something that I started using regularly until a couple of years ago. I used to be intimidated by it. I had no idea how to cut it, let alone use it in a recipe. After my mom raved about my aunt's fennel salad, I gave in and bought some. I quickly realized that fennel was not something I enjoyed eating raw. However, roasted fennel is absolutely amazing because it gives fennel a sweetness that can't be recreated with any other ingredient. This soup is rich and creamy yet tastes like spring. Don't forget the parsley and lemon zest!

1 medium fennel bulb

1¼ lb (560 g) potatoes, peeled

4 tsp (20 ml) olive oil, divided

Salt and pepper

1 medium yellow onion, diced

2 cloves garlic, minced

4 cups (960 ml) vegetable broth

Fresh parsley, for garnish

½ tsp lemon zest, for garnish

Preheat the oven to 350°F (176°C) and line a baking tray with parchment paper. While the oven is preheating, chop the fennel bulb into ½-inch (1.3-cm) thick pieces and cut the potatoes into ½-inch (1.3-cm) dices. Toss the fennel and potato with 2 teaspoons (10 ml) of olive oil and season with salt and pepper. Spread the vegetables evenly on the baking tray and roast in the oven for 25 to 30 minutes. Once the potatoes are cooked, remove the tray from the oven. Set aside a few pieces of fennel and roasted potato in a bowl. These will be used for garnish later.

In a medium stockpot, heat the remaining olive oil over medium heat. Add the onion and sauté for 5 minutes until it becomes translucent. Add the garlic and sauté for 2 minutes until it becomes fragrant. Add the roasted fennel, potatoes and vegetable broth to the stockpot. Bring to a boil, then reduce the heat and allow the soup to simmer for 10 minutes.

Blend the soup using an immersion blender, or in batches when using a regular blender. Season the soup with more salt and pepper to taste.

Serve the soup in bowls and garnish with the reserved fennel and potatoes, fresh parsley and lemon zest.

PER 1 CUP (240 ML) SERVING WITHOUT GARNISHES: CALORIES 206 ⟫⟫ FAT 6.3 G ⟫⟫ CARBOHYDRATES 30.2 G ⟫⟫ FIBER 5.8 G ⟫⟫ PROTEIN 8.3 G

COCONUT MINT PEA SOUP

MAKES 1½ QUARTS (1.4 L)

Coconut, mint and pea are such a delicious combo. My husband actually liked this soup
the best of all the spring soups, which I thought was a bit surprising since he usually prefers hearty soups.

3 cups (720 ml) vegetable broth

1 cup (240 ml) water

1 yellow onion, diced

3 cups (435 g) peas, fresh or frozen

1 (13.5-oz [400-ml]) can coconut milk,
plus more for garnish

2 tbsp (30 ml) fresh lime juice, plus more
to taste

⅓ cup (10 g) chopped mint leaves,
plus more for garnish

Salt and pepper

Add the vegetable broth, water, onion and peas to a pot and bring it to a boil over
medium-high heat. Once it is boiling, reduce the heat and simmer for 10 minutes.
Remove the pot from the heat, add the coconut milk, lime juice and mint before
blending the soup in a blender, or with an immersion blender, until smooth.

The peas are hard to purée completely. If you want an extra smooth soup, strain it
after puréeing it.

Season the soup with salt, pepper and more lime juice to taste. Serve immediately
if you can. It tastes best lukewarm or chilled. Serve with a few fresh mint leaves and
coconut milk drizzle.

PER 1 CUP (240 ML) SERVING WITHOUT GARNISHES: CALORIES 244
FAT 17.2 G ⟫⟫ CARBOHYDRATES 16.9 G ⟫⟫ FIBER 5.9 G ⟫⟫ PROTEIN 8.3 G

FAUX PHO

MAKES 1½ QUARTS (1.4 L)

Traditional pho is made with beef and it takes nearly six hours to make the broth. Since I really don't want either of those things, I've made a much quicker way. Though it may not be as authentic, it is still bursting with flavor and absolutely delicious!

1 tsp black peppercorns

1 cinnamon stick

3 whole cloves

3 cups (720 ml) water

1 star anise

1 yellow onion, roughly diced

1 tsp grated fresh ginger

1 carrot, diced

½ (80 g) fennel bulb, cored

1 bay leaf

1 scallion

½ cup (15 g) cilantro

½ cup (15 g) mint leaves

1 lime

3 oz (85 g) brown rice noodles

2 cups (200 g) mung bean sprouts

2 chilies of choice (bird's eye, jalapeño, red Thai chilies)

1 tbsp (15 ml) soy sauce, plus more to taste

1 lemon

Dry roast the peppercorns, cinnamon and cloves in a pot for 3 minutes, stirring often. Add the water, star anise, onion, ginger, carrot, fennel and bay leaf. If you have any fennel greens left, you can add those now too. Bring all the ingredients in the pot to a boil, then reduce the heat, cover and simmer for 15 minutes.

While the broth is simmering, dice the scallion, chop the herbs and cut the lime into wedges. Bring another pot with water to a boil, add the brown rice noodles and cook for 3 minutes. Divide the noodles between two bowls. Top the bowls with diced scallion, cilantro, mint, sprouts and chilies.

Strain the broth and add the soy sauce. Squeeze the lemon over the broth, adding as much as you like. Add more soy sauce to taste. Pour the broth over the two prepared bowls. Serve immediately with lime wedges.

PER 1 CUP (240 ML) SERVING WITHOUT GARNISHES: CALORIES 99 ⫸⫸ FAT 1.1 G ⫸⫸ CARBOHYDRATES 19.4 G ⫸⫸ FIBER 2.5 G ⫸⫸ PROTEIN 5.0 G

CREAMY SPINACH PEA SOUP

MAKES 1¼ QUARTS (1.2 L)

Chickpeas might be a weird ingredient to see in a creamy soup. However, the same way they are able to turn into a smooth hummus, they can help this green soup become incredibly creamy. Also, don't be discouraged to put Dijon mustard into your soups. Mustard gives this soup just a slight amount of heat that cuts through the deep, earthy spinach and pea flavor.

1 tbsp (15 ml) olive oil, plus more for garnish

1 medium yellow onion, diced

3 cloves garlic, minced

3 cups (720 ml) vegetable broth

2 cups (250 g) frozen or fresh peas

Large handful fresh spinach (3.5 oz [100 g])

1 heaping cup (180 g) soaked and cooked chickpeas or garbanzo beans

½ to 2 tsp (2.5 to 10 ml) Dijon mustard, optional

Salt and pepper

Fresh herbs

In a medium stockpot, heat the olive oil over medium heat. Add the onion and sauté for 5 minutes until it becomes translucent. Add the garlic and sauté for 2 minutes until it becomes fragrant. Add the broth, peas, spinach and chickpeas to the stockpot. Bring to a boil, then reduce the heat and allow the soup to simmer for 10 minutes until the spinach has wilted.

Blend the soup using an immersion blender, or in batches when using a regular blender. Stir ½ teaspoon Dijon mustard into the soup, adding more to taste. Season the soup with salt and pepper to taste.

Serve the soup in bowls with a drizzle of olive oil and a sprinkle of fresh herbs.

PER 1 CUP (240 ML) SERVING WITHOUT GARNISHES: CALORIES 241 ﹥﹥﹥ FAT 6.1 G ﹥﹥﹥ CARBOHYDRATES 34.1 G ﹥﹥﹥ FIBER 10.2 G ﹥﹥﹥ PROTEIN 13.9 G

WATERCRESS SOUP

MAKES 1 QUART (950 ML)

It's a little hard to explain what watercress tastes like if you have never had it before. It has peppery and bitter notes, but can even be a bit spicy. It's slightly similar to radishes and daikon. If you can't find any watercress, then you can substitute arugula instead. It won't have that distinct watercress taste, but will still be a bit peppery.

2 tsp (10 ml) olive oil

1 leek, white and light green parts only, sliced

2 scallions, diced

6½ cups (8 oz [226 g]) chopped watercress, stems trimmed

2 tsp (4 g) chickpea flour or other flour of choice

1 tsp paprika

2 cups (480 ml) vegetable broth

½ cup (120 ml) unsweetened almond milk

Salt and pepper

Heat the olive oil in a pot over medium-high heat and add the leek and scallions. Reserve some of the watercress for garnish and add the rest of it to the pot. Cook for 5 to 7 minutes before stirring the flour and paprika into the pot.

While stirring constantly, slowly add the broth and almond milk. Bring to a boil, then reduce the heat, cover and cook for 10 minutes.

Purée the soup using an immersion blender, or in batches in a blender. For this soup, I don't like to purée it completely. Little flakes of watercress are nice to see throughout the soup. Season the soup with salt and pepper to taste before serving with a garnish of watercress.

PER 1 CUP (240 ML) SERVING WITHOUT GARNISHES: CALORIES 81 ⟫⟫⟫ FAT 4.0 G ⟫⟫⟫ CARBOHYDRATES 6.1 G ⟫⟫⟫ FIBER 2.0 G ⟫⟫⟫ PROTEIN 5.1 G

CREAMY CARAMELIZED ONION SOUP

MAKES 2 QUARTS (1.9 L)

Making caramelized onions can seem like a very daunting task. It should only take about an hour, but it's an hour well spent. There is just no other way to coax out the same amount of flavor and sweetness from an onion.

2 tbsp (30 ml) coconut or olive oil, divided

3 large yellow onions (roughly 24 oz [680 g])

¼ tsp salt

1 tsp balsamic vinegar

1 leek, white and light green parts only, sliced

2 cloves garlic, minced

½ head of cauliflower (roughly 1 lb [454 g]), chopped

½ tsp fresh thyme leaves

2 tbsp (5 g) chopped parsley

3 cups (720 ml) vegetable broth

1 cup (240 ml) unsweetened almond milk

Salt and pepper

Heat 1 tablespoon (15 ml) of oil in a large cast-iron or stainless steel skillet over medium-high heat. Cut the onions into ¼-inch (6-mm) slices. Add the onion to the skillet and cook them, stirring occasionally. After 10 minutes of cooking, sprinkle the salt over the onions and continue to cook. After 20 minutes, you might want to reduce the heat to medium or medium-low and add more oil if the onions are looking very dry.

Be sure not to stir the onions too often. You want them to be able to brown, but also not burn to the bottom of your pan. You'll want to cook the onions for 45 to 60 minutes. Toward the end of your cook time, the onions will stick to the pan quite a bit. Scrape them every minute or two until they become a deep, rich, brown color.

Once the onions are caramelized to your liking, deglaze the pan with balsamic vinegar. Place the caramelized onions in a bowl and set them aside.

Heat 1 tablespoon (15 ml) of oil in a pot and add the leeks, garlic, cauliflower, thyme and parsley. Cook them for 5 minutes before adding the vegetable broth. Bring the broth to a boil then reduce the heat and cook for 10 to 15 minutes until the cauliflower is tender. Add a third of the caramelized onions you prepared to the soup along with the almond milk. Purée the soup until smooth using an immersion blender, or in batches in a blender.

Season the soup with salt and pepper to taste. Serve the soup with the remaining caramelized onions as garnish.

PER 1 CUP (240 ML) SERVING WITHOUT GARNISHES: CALORIES 279 ⟫⟫ FAT 3.1 G ⟫⟫ CARBOHYDRATES 13.6 G ⟫⟫ FIBER 3.7 G ⟫⟫ PROTEIN 4.3 G

FRESH HERB SOUP

MAKES 1 QUART (950 ML)

Sometimes I go to the farmers market and see so many delicious herbs that I have to buy them all. The problem with herbs is that I really shouldn't buy them in bulk. They're obviously not like dried lentils or beans that I can leave in my pantry for months. This soup uses A LOT of herbs. This is great for those moments when I realize I still have a pound (454 g) of herbs that need to be used ASAP or will end up being thrown away.

8 oz (226 g) fresh herbs (any combination of the following: dill, basil, parsley, watercress, chives, oregano, tarragon), divided

2 tsp (10 ml) olive oil

1 yellow onion, finely diced

2 tsp (4 g) chickpea flour (or other flour)

2 cups (480 ml) vegetable broth

¼ cup (60 ml) white wine vinegar

2 cups (480 ml) unsweetened almond milk

Salt and pepper

1 lemon cut into wedges, for garnish

Fresh herbs, chopped, for garnish

Wash the herbs, remove any woody stalks and put them into a food processor. Pulse in order to chop the herbs. Don't pulse too much or you'll end up with a paste.

Heat the olive oil in a pot and add the onion. Cook for 5 minutes, then sprinkle the onion with chickpea flour before adding the vegetable broth, vinegar and almond milk. Whisk the soup as it heats to prevent any flour clumps. Simmer the soup for 5 minutes, then add the chopped herbs while reserving ¼ cup (10 g) of the herbs for later. Simmer for 10 minutes, making sure not to let the soup boil. Season the soup with salt and pepper to taste.

Serve the soup with lemon wedges and a sprinkle of fresh, chopped herbs.

PER 1 CUP (240 ML) SERVING WITHOUT GARNISHES: CALORIES 81 ⟫⟫ FAT 4.9 G ⟫⟫ CARBOHYDRATES 5.4 G ⟫⟫ FIBER 1.4 G ⟫⟫ PROTEIN 3.6 G

TEMPEH TORTILLA SOUP

MAKES 2 QUARTS (1.9 L)

Tortilla soup isn't really known for being healthy. I tried to counteract the not-so-heathy tortillas with lots of veggies and protein-packed chickpeas and tempeh. It's blended into a creamy soup and then topped with all my favorite toppings!

3 (6-inch [15-cm]) whole corn tortillas

3 tbsp (45 ml) coconut oil

7 oz (198 g) tempeh, diced

1 yellow onion, diced

3 cloves garlic, minced

1 tbsp (7 g) paprika

1 tbsp (6 g) cumin

2 tsp (5 g) chili powder

10 oz (283 g) carrots, diced

2 ribs celery, diced

1 lb (454 g) tomatoes, finely diced

4 cups (960 ml) vegetable broth

1 bay leaf

1 cup (70 g) chickpeas, soaked and cooked or rinsed and drained from a can

Salt

½ cup (25 g) chopped, fresh cilantro

1 avocado, diced

Chilies, optional

2 limes cut into wedges

Cut the tortillas in half and then into ¼-inch (6-mm) strips. Heat the coconut oil in a large pot over high heat. Line a large plate with 2 paper towel sheets. Add the tortilla strips, a small handful at a time, to the pot and cook them for a minute until golden brown. Remove them from the pot with a slotted spoon and place them on the paper towel–lined plate. Repeat with the remaining tortilla strips.

Add the diced tempeh to the pot and cook for 3 minutes on each side until the edges turn slightly crispy. Remove from the pot and set aside.

Reduce the heat of the pot and add the onion. Cook the onion for 5 minutes. Add the garlic, spices, carrots, celery and tomatoes to the pot and cook for 10 minutes over medium heat. Add the vegetable broth, bay leaf, chickpeas and a third of the tortilla strips, cover, reduce the heat and simmer for 20 to 30 minutes. Remove the bay leaf and then purée the soup using an immersion blender, or in a blender in batches. Season the soup with salt to taste.

Ladle the soup into bowls. Top each bowl with the remaining tortilla strips, tempeh, cilantro, avocado, chilies (if using) and lime wedges.

PER 1 CUP (240 ML) SERVING WITHOUT GARNISHES: CALORIES 276
FAT 15.2 G   CARBOHYDRATES 26.5 G   FIBER 7.0 G   PROTEIN 11.8 G

GREEN MINESTRONE WITH SPRING VEGETABLES

MAKES 2 QUARTS (1.9 L)

No, this minestrone does not have any pasta in it. I wanted to keep it light and whole-grain pasta tends to be quite heavy. If you really miss the pasta, you can add some; just be sure to add an extra cup (240 ml) of water.

2 tsp (10 ml) olive oil

1 yellow onion, diced

2 cloves garlic, minced

6 fresh mint leaves, chopped

1 scallion, diced

1 rib celery, diced

1 leek, white and light green parts only, sliced

1 fennel bulb, cored and diced

4 cups (960 ml) vegetable broth

1 cup (240 ml) water

2 cups (300 g) chickpeas, soaked and cooked or rinsed and drained from a can

1 cup (150 g) fresh, shelled peas (frozen are fine too)

8 oz (226 g) asparagus, cut into 1-inch (2.5-cm) pieces

½ cup (123 g) Basil Walnut Pesto (page 181), plus more for garnish

¼ cup (6 g) fresh basil

Heat the olive oil in a pot and add the onion. Cook the onion for 5 to 7 minutes. Add the garlic, mint leaves, scallion, celery, leek and fennel to the pot. Cook, stirring occasionally, for 5 minutes. Add the vegetable broth, water and chickpeas. Bring the pot to a boil, reduce the heat and simmer for 10 minutes.

Add the peas and cook for 3 minutes before adding the asparagus and cooking for another 3 minutes. The asparagus should be bright green.

Stir the pesto into the soup. Ladle the soup into bowls and top with an additional teaspoon of pesto and fresh basil.

PER 1 CUP (240 ML) SERVING WITHOUT GARNISHES: CALORIES 201 »»»» FAT 4.3 G »»»» CARBOHYDRATES 30.3 G »»»» FIBER 8.7 G »»»» PROTEIN 11.7 G

COCONUT CARROT SOUP

MAKES 2 QUARTS (1.9 L)

There really is nothing better than a bowl of creamy carrot soup. It's one of my go-to soups. It's quick, made with ingredients I always have at home and, more importantly, toddler approved.

1 tbsp (15 ml) olive oil

1 medium yellow onion, diced

4 cloves garlic, minced

1 tsp grated, fresh ginger

2 lb (900 g) carrots, peeled and diced

4 cups (960 ml) vegetable broth

1 (13.5-oz [400-ml]) can coconut milk

Fresh parsley

Heat the olive oil over medium-high heat in a large pot and add the onion. Cook the onion for 5 to 7 minutes before adding the garlic and ginger. Cook for 2 minutes until the garlic becomes fragrant.

Add the carrots and vegetable broth to the pot and bring them to a boil. Once boiling, reduce the heat, cover and simmer for 15 minutes or until the carrots can easily be pierced with a fork.

Purée the soup with an immersion blender, or in batches in a blender, until smooth. Stir the coconut milk into the soup and serve with fresh parsley.

PER 1 CUP (240 ML) SERVING WITHOUT GARNISHES: CALORIES 191
FAT 12.8 G ⟫⟫ CARBOHYDRATES 16.3 G ⟫⟫ FIBER 4.2 G ⟫⟫ PROTEIN 4.8 G

RUSTIC NEW POTATO STEW

MAKES 2 QUARTS (1.9 L)

You can buy potatoes all year but they will vary in type and size throughout. In spring, you'll see lots of new potatoes, or what some like to call baby potatoes. New potatoes are smaller because they have been dug up early to make room for other potatoes to grow larger and mature. These little potatoes are sweeter and thin-skinned. I like adding them whole to this stew. If you come across one that is a bit too large, just cut it in half.

2 tsp (10 ml) olive oil

1 yellow onion, diced

2 cloves garlic, minced

8 cups (1.9 L) vegetable broth

1 bay leaf

1 lb (453 g) new potatoes

1 rib celery, diced

2 carrots, diced

1 scallion, diced

1 cup (100 g) fresh peas (or frozen is fine)

Salt and pepper

¼ cup (15 g) parsley, chopped

3 sprigs fresh dill, chopped

Heat the olive oil in a large pot and add the diced onion. Cook the onion for 5 to 7 minutes before adding the garlic. Cook for 2 more minutes, then add the vegetable broth, bay leaf, new potatoes, celery, carrots and scallion. Bring to a boil and then reduce the heat and simmer, uncovered, for 20 to 30 minutes until the potatoes are tender.

While the soup is simmering, shell your fresh peas. Add the peas once the potatoes are tender. Cook for 3 minutes, then season the soup with salt and pepper to taste. Remove the pot from the heat and stir in the fresh parsley and dill.

PER 1 CUP (240 ML) SERVING WITHOUT GARNISHES: CALORIES 116 FAT 2.7 G CARBOHYDRATES 15.7 G FIBER 3.0 G PROTEIN 7.2 G

RAW CARROT SOUP

MAKES 3 CUPS (720 ML)

If you haven't delved into the world of raw or cold soups, it's about time.
It can take a bit of getting used to, but it's a nice, refreshing change.

2 carrots, roughly 7 oz (200 g)

1 rib celery

1 cup (165 g) diced mango

3-inch (7.6-cm) piece leek, pale section only

1 cup (240 ml) water

1 tbsp (12 g) almond butter

1 tbsp (15 ml) lemon juice

⅛ tsp salt

Microgreens

Hazelnuts

Olive oil

Roughly chop the carrots and celery. Add all of the ingredients, except the microgreens, hazelnuts and olive oil, in a high-powered blender and blend until smooth. If your blender isn't able to handle such big chunks of raw carrot, grate them and the celery first.

Season the soup with more salt if needed. Chop the hazelnuts and rinse off the microgreens. Serve the raw soup cold, with a sprinkle of microgreens, some chopped hazelnuts and a drizzle of olive oil.

PER 1 CUP (240 ML) SERVING WITHOUT GARNISHES: CALORIES 121 ⟫⟫ FAT 3.4 G ⟫⟫ CARBOHYDRATES 22.4 G ⟫⟫ FIBER 3.8 G ⟫⟫ PROTEIN 2.6 G

CELERIAC ARUGULA SOUP WITH COCONUT CREAM AND CRISPY CHICKPEAS

MAKES 2 QUARTS (1.9 L)

This soup is good. It's amazing, though, once you add the coconut cream and crispy chickpeas! Any leftover crispy chickpeas are always a great snack.

1 celeriac

2 tsp (10 ml) olive oil

1 yellow onion, diced

5 cups (1.2 L) vegetable broth

1 cup (240 ml) Whipped Coconut Cream (page 180)

2 packed cups (80 g) arugula

Salt and pepper

CRISPY CHICKPEAS

1½ cups (240 g) chickpeas, soaked and cooked (or rinsed and drained from a can)

1 tbsp (15 ml) olive oil

1 tbsp (8 g) nutritional yeast

½ tsp garlic powder

1 tsp paprika

¼ tsp salt

Preheat the oven to 375°F (190°C) and line a baking sheet with parchment paper.

Peel the celeriac and dice it. Heat the olive oil in a pot and add the diced onion and celeriac to it. Cook for 7 minutes while stirring occasionally. Add the vegetable broth to the pot and bring it to a boil. Once boiling, reduce the heat and simmer for 20 minutes until the celeriac is tender.

While the soup is cooking, prepare the whipped coconut cream and crispy chickpeas. The trick to making crispy chickpeas is to ensure that the chickpeas are thoroughly dried. Dry off your chickpeas on a paper towel. Transfer them to a bowl and mix them together with the olive oil, nutritional yeast, garlic powder, paprika and salt. Spread them on the baking sheet and roast them in the oven for 25 to 30 minutes, stirring once halfway through.

Remove the pot from the heat and add the arugula. Purée the soup using an immersion blender, or in a blender in batches, until smooth. Season with salt and pepper to taste. Serve the soup with a dollop of coconut cream and some crispy chickpeas.

PER 1 CUP (240 ML) SERVING WITHOUT GARNISHES: CALORIES 187 ⟫⟫⟫ FAT 6.8 G ⟫⟫⟫ CARBOHYDRATES 22.8 G ⟫⟫⟫ FIBER 6.1 G ⟫⟫⟫ PROTEIN 9.9 G

SPICY ORANGE CARROT SOUP

MAKES 2 QUARTS (1.9 L)

This is the adult version of my go-to Coconut Carrot Soup (page 127). I don't get to make this soup nearly as much as I would like. With a lot of spicy soups, you can just omit the spicy ingredient, but with this soup, it really doesn't work unfortunately. If you omit the cayenne peppers, the sweetness from the carrots, orange and coconut milk is too much. The sweet-spicy balance is perfect in this soup. You really don't want to mess with it.

2 tsp (10 ml) olive oil

1 yellow onion, diced

1 cayenne pepper, diced (you can add 2, if you are really adventurous)

1 tbsp (7 g) ground cumin

1 lb (454 g) carrots, diced

1 lb (454 g) cauliflower, diced

Juice and pulp from 1 orange (should equal roughly ⅓ cup [79 ml])

4 cups (960 ml) vegetable broth

1 (13.5-oz [400-ml]) can coconut milk

¼ cup (6 g) fresh basil

⅛ cup (18 g) sesame seeds

Heat the olive oil in a pot and add the diced onion and cayenne pepper. Cook for 5 minutes. Add the cumin, carrots and cauliflower and cook for 5 more minutes. Use a citrus reamer to get the juice and pulp out of the orange. Add the vegetable broth, orange juice and pulp to the pot. Bring the soup to a boil, reduce the heat and simmer for 20 to 30 minutes until the carrots and cauliflower are very tender.

Purée the soup with an immersion blender, or in batches in a blender. If the carrot and cauliflower are still grainy, add the soup back to the pot and cook for another 10 minutes before puréeing again. Stir the coconut milk into the soup and allow it to simmer for 5 minutes.

Serve with a few fresh basil leaves and a sprinkle of sesame seeds.

PER 1 CUP (240 ML) SERVING WITHOUT GARNISHES: CALORIES 196
FAT 14.2 G   CARBOHYDRATES 14.6 G   FIBER 4.3 G   PROTEIN 5.5 G

LEMON ORZO SOUP WITH PEAS AND SPINACH

MAKES 2 QUARTS (1.9 L)

This orzo soup is simple to make and one of my kids' favorites.
They love the peas, the whole grain orzo and the bright lemon taste.

1 tbsp (15 ml) olive oil

1 medium yellow onion, diced

2 cloves garlic, minced

5 cups (1.2 L) vegetable broth

2 cups (480 ml) water

¼ cup (60 ml) fresh lemon juice

Small handful fresh dill

Small handful of parsley, plus more for garnish

1½ cups (190 g) peas

2 cups (380 g) whole grain orzo

Large handful fresh spinach (3.5 oz [100 g])

In a medium stockpot, heat the olive oil over medium heat. Add the onion and cook for 5 minutes until it becomes translucent. Add the garlic and cook for 2 minutes until it becomes fragrant. Add the broth, water, lemon juice, dill, parsley, peas and orzo to the stockpot.

Bring the soup to a boil, then reduce the heat and allow it to simmer for at least 10 minutes, stirring occasionally to prevent the orzo from sticking together. Orzo cooking times vary slightly depending on the brand. Cook until the orzo has a firm and slightly chewy texture. Stir in the fresh spinach and cook for 2 to 4 minutes until the spinach becomes bright green and starts wilting.

Serve the soup in bowls and garnish with fresh parsley.

PER 1 CUP (240 ML) SERVING WITHOUT GARNISHES: CALORIES 239 ⁙⁙ FAT 3.7 G ⁙⁙ CARBOHYDRATES 41.8 G ⁙⁙ FIBER 3.5 G ⁙⁙ PROTEIN 10.9 G

LEMON CILANTRO SPINACH SOUP

MAKES 3 CUPS (720 ML)

I wanted to keep this soup really simple so that the cilantro and spinach could shine through.
If it's too light for your liking, you can always add some coconut or almond milk.

1 tbsp (15 ml) olive oil

1 medium yellow onion, diced

2 cloves garlic, minced

3 cups (720 ml) vegetable broth

¼ cup (60 ml) lemon juice

1 cup (50 g) chopped cilantro, leaves and stems, plus more for garnish

Large handful fresh baby spinach (3.5 oz [100 g])

Salt and pepper

Homemade Croutons (page 184)

In a medium stockpot, heat the olive oil over medium heat. Add the onion and sauté for 5 minutes until it becomes translucent. Add the garlic and sauté for 2 minutes until the garlic becomes fragrant. Add the broth, lemon juice, cilantro and spinach to the stockpot. Bring to a boil, then reduce the heat and allow the soup to simmer for 10 minutes, stirring occasionally.

Blend the soup using an immersion blender, or in batches when using a regular blender. Season the soup with salt and pepper to taste. Add the croutons to the soup and garnish with chopped cilantro.

PER 1 CUP (240 ML) SERVING WITHOUT GARNISHES: CALORIES 110 ⋙ FAT 6.4 G ⋙ CARBOHYDRATES 6.8 G ⋙ FIBER 1.8 G ⋙ PROTEIN 6.6 G

LIGHT AND REFRESHING SUMMER SOUPS

For some reason, people often believe that summer and soup can't coexist. Yes, soup definitely isn't the first thing that comes to mind when I think of summer food. However, during the summer there is an overwhelming amount of produce that is begging to be made into soup.

While a lot of the soups in this chapter are cold or chilled, there are a few warm ones. One of these is the Roasted Tomato Soup (page 146). It tastes infinitely better made with fresh, seasonal tomatoes than with tomatoes that have been stored for weeks and grown indoors during the winter months.

I did try to keep time in mind for these summer soups. Almost all of them don't require a lot of cook time so that you can get in and out of the kitchen quickly without overheating.

WHAT'S IN SEASON

BEETS – BELL PEPPERS – BERRIES – CORN – CUCUMBER – EGGPLANT –
MELONS – OKRA – SUMMER SQUASH – TOMATOES – ZUCCHINI

RAW AVOCADO CUCUMBER SOUP

MAKES ABOUT 1½ CUPS (360 ML)

This is one of my favorite soups to make in the summertime. It is quick, requires no heating and is refreshing at the same time. The avocado gives the soup a creamy texture while still keeping it light.

1 avocado

1 cucumber, chopped

5 sprigs fresh dill

5 tbsp (75 ml) fresh lemon juice (from 2 lemons)

Salt and pepper, to taste

2 tbsp (30 ml) Whipped Coconut Cream (page 180), optional

Cut the avocado in half, remove the pit and add the scooped avocado pulp to a food processor or blender. Add the cucumber, dill and lemon juice as well and blend until smooth. Adjust the salt and pepper according to taste.

Pour the soup into bowls and serve cold with a dollop of whipped coconut cream.

PER 1 CUP (240ML) SERVING WITHOUT GARNISHES: CALORIES 316 ⟫⟫ FAT 26.8 G ⟫⟫ CARBOHYDRATES 19.9 G ⟫⟫ FIBER 10.2 G ⟫⟫ PROTEIN 4.3 G

GAZPACHO

The better your tomatoes are, the better your gazpacho will taste. There really isn't a point in making gazpacho unless you can get fragrant, seasonal tomatoes. Heirloom tomatoes are best for this, and if they are from your own garden, even better!

½ cucumber (200 g)

1 red bell pepper

1 green bell pepper

1 scallion

1 clove garlic

1 lb (454 g) tomatoes

2 tsp (10 ml) white wine vinegar

Salt and pepper

2 tsp (10 ml) olive oil

¼ cup (15 g) fresh parsley, chopped

Add the cucumber, bell peppers, scallion, garlic, tomatoes and white wine vinegar to a food processor. Pulse and blend until your desired consistency is reached. Some like their gazpacho fairly chunky while others like it almost smooth. Season the gazpacho with salt and pepper to taste.

Serve it immediately in bowls with a drizzle of olive oil and chopped parsley.

PER 1 CUP (240 ML) SERVING WITHOUT GARNISHES: CALORIES 50 ⟫⟫ FAT 0.5 G ⟫⟫ CARBOHYDRATES 11.3 G ⟫⟫ FIBER 2.5 G ⟫⟫ PROTEIN 2.0 G

WATERMELON GAZPACHO

MAKES 1 QUART (950 ML)

If you like traditional gazpacho, then watermelon gazpacho is definitely worth a try. The watermelon makes this gazpacho a bit sweeter, but also lighter and more refreshing. I prefer eating it as a first course or light lunch on hot days when I can't be bothered to turn on the stove.

4 heaping cups (650 g) diced, seedless watermelon, divided

1 small red onion

4 Roma tomatoes

1 red bell pepper

Handful of cilantro, plus more for garnish

1 cucumber, chopped

1 tsp (5 ml) white wine vinegar

Salt and pepper to taste

½ an avocado, sliced

Blend 3½ cups (563 g) of the watermelon, red onion, tomatoes, bell pepper, cilantro, cucumber and white wine vinegar to a food processor or blender.

Season the gazpacho with salt and pepper to taste. Serve the watermelon gazpacho chilled with the remaining ½ cup (80 g) of diced watermelon, extra cilantro and sliced avocado as garnish.

PER 1 CUP (240 ML) SERVING WITHOUT GARNISHES: CALORIES 103 ⇝ FAT 0.6 G ⇝ CARBOHYDRATES 24.6 G ⇝ FIBER 3.5 G ⇝ PROTEIN 3.1 G

ROASTED TOMATO SOUP

MAKES 1 QUART (950 ML)

A lot of people wait for the colder months to make tomato soups. Tomatoes in the summer are so incredibly good, and it's a shame if you don't use them to make a tomato soup. The oven does all the work for you in this recipe so you don't have to spend any time in front of the stove. Once the tomatoes are roasted to perfection, just blitz them with some water in a food processor for your finished tomato soup. Easy!

2 lb (907 g) Roma tomatoes

4 cloves garlic

2 yellow onions, diced

5 oregano sprigs or ½ tsp dried oregano

4 thyme sprigs or ½ tsp dried thyme

2 rosemary sprigs or ¼ tsp dried rosemary

½ cup (120 ml) olive oil

1½ cups (360 ml) hot water

¼ tsp salt

Fresh cracked pepper

Fresh basil

Homemade Croutons (page 184)

Preheat the oven to 395°F (200°C). Quarter the tomatoes and garlic. Place them along with the onions in a large, shallow baking dish. Lay the fresh herbs on top of the tomatoes. Drizzle generously with the olive oil. Bake in the oven for 40 minutes.

Remove the baking dish from the oven and wait 10 minutes. Toss the herbs and add the tomatoes, garlic, onions, water and salt to a food processor without the oil at the bottom of the baking dish. Pulse to purée the tomatoes. Season with more salt to taste.

Serve the soup with fresh cracked pepper, basil and homemade croutons.

PER 1 CUP (240 ML) SERVING WITHOUT GARNISHES: CALORIES 312 ››››› FAT 29.0 G ››››› CARBOHYDRATES 15.2 G ››››› FIBER 4.1 G ››››› PROTEIN 2.8 G

CHILLED AVOCADO MINT SOUP

MAKES 1 QUART (950 ML)

Whenever I make this quick soup, it's really hard to let it chill. It already tastes so good when it's warm. Waiting is worth it, though. I promise!

1 tsp coconut oil

2 scallions, diced

1 clove garlic, minced

3 cups (720 ml) vegetable broth

1 avocado

¼ cup (5 g) chopped, fresh mint leaves, plus more for garnish

1 tbsp (15 ml) fresh lime juice

Salt

½ cup (120 ml) coconut milk

Heat the coconut oil in a pot over medium-high heat. Add the scallions and garlic and cook for 3 minutes. Add the vegetable broth, avocado and mint. Reduce the heat and simmer for 5 minutes. Purée the soup using an immersion blender, or in a blender in batches. If you'd like, you can strain the soup to remove any mint leaves. Stir the lime juice into the soup and season with salt to taste.

Chill the soup in the fridge for at least an hour. Serve with a drizzle of coconut milk and fresh mint leaves.

PER 1 CUP (240 ML) SERVING WITHOUT GARNISHES: CALORIES 148 ⫸ FAT 12.0 G ⫸ CARBOHYDRATES 6.4 G ⫸ FIBER 4.0 G ⫸ PROTEIN 5.0 G

OKRA CURRY SOUP

MAKES 1 QUART (950 ML)

Okra can get slimy very quickly if you let it cook for too long. All too often, I forget to keep an eye on the clock when I'm cooking. With okra, I make sure to pay attention. Keeping the okra whole prevents you from overcooking it too fast. If the okra pieces are too big for you though, you can dice them instead.

1 tsp cumin

1 tsp ground coriander

1 tsp mustard seeds

1 tsp turmeric

2 tsp (10 ml) coconut oil

1 yellow onion, diced

2 cloves garlic, minced

1 tsp grated, fresh ginger

20 pieces okra, tops removed

1 tomato, finely diced

1 cup (240 ml) water

1 (13.5-oz [400-ml]) can coconut milk

½ tsp salt

1 tbsp (15 ml) fresh lime juice

Dry roast the cumin, coriander, mustard seeds and turmeric for 3 minutes in a large pot over high heat while stirring constantly. Reduce the heat to medium-low and add the coconut oil and onion. Cook the onion for 5 minutes before adding the garlic, ginger, okra and tomatoes.

Cook the okra for 5 minutes, stirring often. Be careful not to mush the okra when you stir it. Add the water, coconut milk and salt. Bring everything to a boil and cook for 5 minutes until the okra has softened. Stir the lime juice into the soup and season with more salt to taste.

PER 1 CUP (240 ML) SERVING WITHOUT GARNISHES: CALORIES 304 ››››
FAT 27.1 G ›››› CARBOHYDRATES 15.3 G ›››› FIBER 5.5 G ›››› PROTEIN 4.5 G

CHILLED CANTALOUPE SOUP

MAKES 2½ CUPS (600 ML)

Other than the watermelon gazpacho, I'm not really one for fruity soups. This cantaloupe soup is another exception though. Be sure that your cantaloupe is ripe or it won't have a sweet taste.

2 cups (320 g) diced cantaloupe

½ cup (120 ml) unsweetened oat milk (unsweetened rice, soy or almond works as well)

½ cup (120 ml) water

6 fresh mint leaves, plus more for garnish

1 apple, peeled and cored

Pinch of salt

Add all of the ingredients to a blender and blend until smooth. Strain the soup through a sieve, removing any unblended mint leaves. Season the soup with more salt to taste.

Chill the soup in the fridge for at least an hour. Serve it with a few fresh mint leaves.

PER 1 CUP (240 ML) SERVING WITHOUT GARNISHES: CALORIES 90 ⟫⟫ FAT 1.1 G ⟫⟫ CARBOHYDRATES 21.2 G ⟫⟫ FIBER 3.3 G ⟫⟫ PROTEIN 1.3 G

LOADED TACO SOUP

MAKES 2 QUARTS (1.9 L)

Chili, taco soup, is there really a difference? I like to think so. All those goodies you would load your taco with are in or on this soup. Don't forget to make the vegan cheddar cheese sauce for this recipe!

2 tsp (10 ml) olive oil

1 yellow onion, diced

4 cloves garlic, minced

1 tbsp (7 g) ground cumin

1 tbsp (8 g) paprika

1 tbsp (8 g) smoked paprika

2 tsp (4 g) chili powder

1 tsp dried oregano

3 bell peppers (red, green, yellow or orange), diced

1 zucchini, diced

2 cups (344 g) beans (kidney, black, pinto or garbanzo, soaked and cooked [or drained and rinsed from a can])

1 cup (172 g) black beans, soaked and cooked (or drained and rinsed from a can)

2 Roma tomatoes, diced

4 cups (960 ml) water

1 tsp salt

2 tbsp (30 g) tomato paste, optional

Whole corn tortilla chips, for topping

Vegan Cheddar Cheese Sauce (page 186), for topping

Vegan Sour Cream (page 180), for topping

Fresh Garlic Cilantro Salsa (page 186), for topping

1 small head romaine lettuce, chopped, for topping

1 jalapeño, sliced, for topping

Fresh cilantro, chopped, for topping

Heat the olive oil in a large pot. Add the onion and cook for 5 to 7 minutes until it starts to turn translucent. Add the garlic, cumin, paprika, smoked paprika, chili powder, oregano, peppers and zucchini. Cook for 3 minutes, coating all of the vegetables in the spices.

Add the beans, tomatoes, water and salt. Bring the soup to a boil over high heat, and then reduce the heat and simmer, covered, for 20 minutes. Remove the lid and cook for 10 more minutes. Season the soup with salt to taste. If the soup isn't thick enough for you, you can add tomato paste.

Ladle the taco soup into large bowls, leaving enough room for plenty of toppings. Use some of the toppings listed or add your favorite taco toppings to the soup.

PER 1 CUP (240 ML) SERVING WITHOUT GARNISHES: CALORIES 143 ⟫⟫ FAT 2.3 G ⟫⟫ CARBOHYDRATES 26.0 G ⟫⟫ FIBER 7.2 G ⟫⟫ PROTEIN 7.5 G

CREAMY CORN CHOWDER

MAKES 2 QUARTS (1.9 L)

The best thing you can do with fresh corn is grill it and eat it lightly salted. However, this creamy corn chowder is the next best thing you can make with fresh corn. It's oil-free and much lighter than your typical chowder. Canned corn can also work in this chowder if you're in a pinch.

4 cups (960 ml) vegetable broth

1 yellow onion, diced

2 ribs celery

1 tsp chopped fresh thyme or ½ tsp dried thyme

1 lb (454 g) potatoes, diced

2 cups (280 g) fresh corn kernels

1 red bell pepper, diced

½ tsp salt

2 tbsp (12 g) chickpea flour

3 cups (720 ml) unsweetened almond milk

Salt and pepper

Add the broth, onion, celery, thyme and potatoes to a pot. Bring the broth to a boil, reduce the heat and simmer, covered, for 15 minutes. Add the corn, bell pepper and salt to the pot. Cook the chowder for 5 minutes.

In a separate bowl, whisk the chickpea flour with the almond milk and slowly add it to the chowder. Cook the chowder for 5 more minutes, stirring often. Season the chowder with salt and pepper to taste before serving.

PER 1 CUP (240 ML) SERVING WITHOUT GARNISHES: CALORIES 142 ⇒⇒⇒ FAT 2.9 G ⇒⇒⇒ CARBOHYDRATES 24.7 G ⇒⇒⇒ FIBER 4.3 G ⇒⇒⇒ PROTEIN 6.4 G

EDAMAME MISO SOUP

MAKES 3 CUPS (720 ML)

Who doesn't love edamame? Get a whole lot of it in this easy miso soup. Spinach is added for an extra vitamin boost, and don't skip the chopped scallions!

1 tbsp (5 g) wakame seaweed
2 tbsp (40 g) vegan miso paste
2¼ cups (540 ml) water, divided
1 cup (100 g) shelled edamame
⅛ cup (10 g) chopped, fresh ginger
½ cup (15 g) baby spinach
1 scallion, chopped, for garnish

Soak the wakame seaweed for 5 minutes in a bit of water to rehydrate it. Drain the water from the seaweed and set it aside. Dissolve the miso paste in ¼ cup (60 ml) of water.

Bring 2 cups (473 ml) of water to a boil in a stockpot, and add the edamame and ginger. Cook for 4 minutes until the edamame is cooked. Stir the baby spinach into the pot and remove it from the stove. Add the soaked wakame and miso water.

Divide the soup into bowls, garnish with chopped scallion and serve immediately.

PER 1 CUP (240 ML) SERVING WITHOUT GARNISHES: CALORIES 86 ⟫⟩ FAT 2.8 G ⟫⟩ CARBOHYDRATES 10.0 G ⟫⟩ FIBER 2.9 G ⟫⟩ PROTEIN 6.3 G

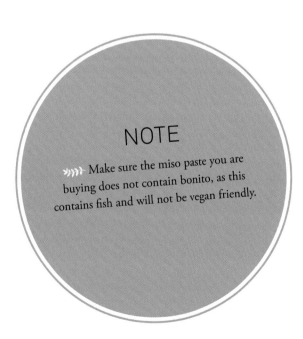

NOTE

⟫⟩ Make sure the miso paste you are buying does not contain bonito, as this contains fish and will not be vegan friendly.

GARLIC EGGPLANT "MEATBALLS" IN BROTH

MAKES 16 MEATBALLS

My boys do not like eggplant. No matter what I use eggplant in, they refuse to eat it because of its texture. These "meatballs" are the only thing that I've been able to hide eggplant from them in. When you take them out of the oven, they will seem fairly dry, but the dryness will help them to soak up lots of broth without falling apart.

1 eggplant, peeled and diced

4 cloves garlic

¾ cup (22 g) fresh parsley, divided

1 cup (50 g) nutritional yeast

¼ tsp salt, plus more to taste

4 oz (110 g) day-old, whole grain bread

½ cup (120 ml) unsweetened almond milk

1 jalapeño, optional

⅓ cup (50 g) chickpea flour

2 tsp (10 ml) olive oil

6 cups (1.4 L) vegetable broth

1 cup (15 g) fresh spinach

Preheat the oven to 375°F (190°C) and line a baking tray with parchment paper.

Add the diced eggplant, garlic, ½ cup (15 g) of parsley, nutritional yeast, salt, bread and almond milk to a food processor. Pulse the mixture until no big chunks are left. It shouldn't be puréed though. The mixture will appear very wet. Scrape the eggplant mixture into a bowl.

Finely dice the jalapeño, if using. I like these with a little bit of heat and the jalapeño also gives these otherwise brown meatballs just a bit of color. Add the chickpea flour at this time as well.

The mixture will still be moist, but you should be able to roll it into 16 tablespoon-size (15 g) balls. Place the meatballs on the lined baking tray. Brush the meatballs with olive oil and sprinkle a bit of salt on each one. Bake them in the oven for 8 to 10 minutes. At this point, the bottoms should be browned. Flip each meatball and bake for 5 more minutes.

Heat the vegetable broth on the stove. Stir in the spinach and let it wilt before ladling the broth into bowls and adding a few meatballs to each. Top with the remaining fresh parsley.

PER 1 (4 MEATBALLS AND BROTH) SERVING WITHOUT GARNISHES: CALORIES 206 ⋙ FAT 5.4 G ⋙ CARBOHYDRATES 32.9 G ⋙ FIBER 11.2 G ⋙ PROTEIN 11.8 G

CHILLED BORSCHT

MAKES 2 QUARTS (1.9 L)

This cold, gorgeous-looking soup is perfect on hot summer days. The cucumber makes this borscht refreshing and light.

1 large beet
2 cups (480 ml) unsweetened almond milk
2 tbsp (30 ml) apple cider vinegar
1 cucumber
2 scallions, diced
½ cup (5 g) chopped, fresh dill
1 cup (240 ml) water
Salt and pepper

Clean the beet under warm water and peel it. Steam the beet in a steamer basket for 15 to 30 minutes. The time it takes to steam a beet will vary. The beet is cooked once you can easily pierce it with a knife. Remove the beet and plunge it in cold water. After 3 minutes, remove the beet and dice it. Set it aside.

Prepare a vegan "buttermilk" by whisking together the almond milk and apple cider vinegar until foamy. Let the buttermilk mixture stand for at least 10 minutes.

While the buttermilk is resting, finely dice the cucumber and scallions and chop the dill.

Add the water, diced beet, cucumber, dill and scallion to the buttermilk and mix gently with a spoon. Season with salt and pepper to taste. Chill the borscht in the fridge for an hour before serving.

PER 1 CUP (240 ML) SERVING WITHOUT GARNISHES: CALORIES 31 »»» FAT 1.1 G »»» CARBOHYDRATES 5.1 G »»» FIBER 1.2 G »»» PROTEIN 1.4 G

SUMMER VEGETABLE CURRY SOUP

MAKES 1½ QUARTS (1.4 L)

There are those rainy summer days where I still crave a good Thai curry. I like using seasonal vegetables in the curry such as zucchini and summer squash. Even though those aren't traditional Thai vegetables, they still work really well in this dish.

1 tsp coconut oil

2 tbsp (30 g) red Thai curry paste (yellow or green curry paste will work too)

2 cloves garlic, minced

2 tsp (10 g) grated, fresh ginger

1 summer squash, sliced

1 zucchini, sliced

1 red bell pepper, sliced

2 cups (480 ml) water

1 (13.5-oz [400-ml]) can coconut milk

1 packed cup (40 g) fresh spinach, chopped

Salt

1 lime cut into wedges, for garnish

15 basil leaves, for garnish

Heat the coconut oil and curry paste in a large pot. Add the garlic, ginger, squash, zucchini and bell pepper. Cook the vegetables over medium heat for 5 minutes, stirring often.

Add the water and coconut milk. Bring the soup to a boil, then reduce the heat and simmer for 10 minutes. Stir the spinach into the soup and cook for 1 minute until the spinach begins to wilt.

Season the soup with salt to taste. Cut the lime into wedges. Serve it with lime wedges and basil.

PER 1 CUP (240 ML) SERVING WITHOUT GARNISHES: CALORIES 192 ⋙ FAT 18.0 G ⋙ CARBOHYDRATES 8.8 G ⋙ FIBER 2.7 G ⋙ PROTEIN 2.9 G

JALAPEÑO BASIL SOUP

MAKES 2½ CUPS (600 ML)

This soup is not kid-approved. This is the type of light appetizer soup you want to be having while slurping on some margaritas. No kids in sight!

2 cups (40 g) fresh basil

2 cups (480 ml) unsweetened almond milk

1 tbsp (15 ml) apple cider vinegar

1 small jalapeño

4 cherry tomatoes, diced

BASIL BREADCRUMBS
2 slices crusty, whole grain bread

½ cup (12 g) chopped, fresh basil

Salt

Blend the basil, almond milk, apple cider vinegar and jalapeño together until smooth. Set aside while you make the basil breadcrumbs.

Add the bread, basil and salt to a food processor and pulse until crumbled.

Serve the soup cold with a sprinkle of basil breadcrumbs and diced cherry tomatoes.

PER 1 CUP (240 ML) SERVING WITHOUT GARNISHES: CALORIES 39 ⟩⟩⟩ FAT 2.9 G ⟩⟩⟩ CARBOHYDRATES 2.4 G ⟩⟩⟩ FIBER 1.2 G ⟩⟩⟩ PROTEIN 1.4 G

TRI-COLORED BELL PEPPER SOUP WITH MILLET

MAKES 1½ QUARTS (1.4 L)

Having light summer soups is always nice. Sometimes, though, I need a little extra something in my soup to give me a push of energy. The millet in this recipe does just that. If you don't have millet on hand, you can use quinoa, whole grain bulgur or even brown rice as a substitute.

1 red bell pepper

1 yellow bell pepper

1 green bell pepper

2 tsp (10 ml) olive oil

2 cloves garlic, minced

2 tomatoes, peeled and diced

4 cups (960 ml) vegetable broth

1 cup (200 g) uncooked millet

2 cups (473 ml) water

1 tsp chopped, fresh thyme or ½ tsp dried thyme

Cayenne pepper, optional

Salt and pepper

Use a peeler to peel the skin off the bell peppers. Seed and dice the bell peppers. Set a quarter of the bell peppers aside.

Heat the olive oil in a pot over medium-high heat. Add the garlic and diced bell peppers. Cook for 3 minutes, until the garlic is very fragrant. Add the tomatoes and broth and let the soup simmer for 20 minutes.

Meanwhile, cook the millet. Rinse the millet under cold water. Add the millet and water to a pot and bring to a boil. Once boiling, reduce the heat and simmer for 20 minutes on low. Fluff the millet with a fork. Add the bell peppers you set aside earlier to the millet. Mix the thyme and cayenne pepper to the millet as well. Season the millet with salt and pepper to taste.

Once the soup is done cooking, purée it with an immersion blender, or in batches in a blender, until smooth. Season the soup with salt and pepper to taste. Serve the soup with a scoop of the prepared millet.

PER 1 CUP (240 ML) SERVING WITHOUT GARNISHES: CALORIES 201 ⟫⟫ FAT 4.2 G ⟫⟫ CARBOHYDRATES 33 G ⟫⟫ FIBER 4.5 G ⟫⟫ PROTEIN 8.2 G

CHUNKY JALAPEÑO TORTILLA SOUP

MAKES 2 QUARTS (1.9 L)

This is definitely a tortilla soup with some heat. I left this tortilla soup chunky because that's what I prefer in the summer. If that's too many vegetables looking at you for a tortilla soup, then you can definitely purée it.

3 (6-inch [15-cm]) whole corn tortillas

3 tbsp (45 ml) coconut oil

1 yellow onion, diced

3 cloves garlic, minced

1 tbsp (6 g) paprika

1 tbsp (6 g) cumin

2 tsp (4 g) chili powder

2 jalapeños, deseeded and diced

1 green bell pepper, diced

1 red bell pepper, diced

1 lb (454 g) tomatoes, finely diced

3 cups (720 ml) vegetable broth

1 bay leaf

2 cups (350 g) kidney beans, soaked and cooked (or rinsed and drained from a can)

Salt

½ cup (8 g) fresh, chopped cilantro, for garnish

1 avocado, diced, for garnish

2 limes cut into wedges, for garnish

Cut the tortillas in half and then into ¼-inch (6-mm) strips. Heat the coconut oil in a large pot over high heat. Line a large plate with 2 paper towel sheets. Add the tortilla strips, a small handful at a time, to the pot and cook them for a minute until golden brown. Remove them from the pot with a slotted spoon and place them on the paper towel–lined plate. Repeat with the remaining tortilla strips.

Reduce the heat of the pot and add the onion. Cook the onion for 5 minutes. Add the garlic, spices, jalapeños, bell peppers and tomatoes to the pot and cook for 10 minutes over medium heat. Add the vegetable broth, bay leaf and beans, cover, reduce the heat and simmer for 20 to 30 minutes. Remove the bay leaf and season the soup with salt to taste.

Divide a third of the prepared tortilla strips between bowls. Ladle the soup into each bowl. Top each bowl with the remaining tortilla strips, cilantro, avocado and lime wedges.

PER 1 CUP (240 ML) SERVING WITHOUT GARNISHES: CALORIES 143 ⟫⟫ FAT 6.4 G ⟫⟫ CARBOHYDRATES 16.8 G ⟫⟫ FIBER 4.3 G ⟫⟫ PROTEIN 6.6 G

15-MINUTE SUMMER VEGETABLE STEW

MAKES 2 QUARTS (1.9 L)

Summer is no time to be spending hours over the stove. But I still want a comforting bowl of stew sometimes. The use of tomato paste lets us cheat hours out of this stew.

8 cups (1.9 L) vegetable broth

1 lb (454 g) tomatoes, diced

1 cup (182 g) cannellini beans, soaked and cooked (or drained and rinsed from a can)

2 cloves garlic, minced

2 zucchini, diced

1 yellow bell pepper, diced

1 tbsp (3 g) fresh oregano leaves

½ cup (120 g) tomato paste

Salt and pepper

¼ cup (6 g) fresh basil, for garnish

Heat the vegetable broth and tomatoes in large pot over medium-high heat. Add the beans, garlic, zucchini, bell pepper, oregano and tomato paste. Simmer the stew for 10 minutes.

Season the stew with salt and pepper to taste before serving with some fresh basil leaves.

PER 1 CUP (240 ML) SERVING WITHOUT GARNISHES: CALORIES 144 »»» FAT 1.9 G »»» CARBOHYDRATES 21.5 G »»» FIBER 7.3 G »»» PROTEIN 11.6 G

CREAMY CUCUMBER AVOCADO SOUP

MAKES 1¼ QUARTS (1.2 L)

This soup is silky smooth. It tastes very rich but light at the same time. It's perfect for those hot summer days when I don't want to spend more than five minutes in the kitchen.

1 avocado, diced

½ cucumber, peeled and chopped

1 scallion, diced

2 cups (480 ml) vegetable broth

1 (13.5-oz [400-ml]) can coconut milk

2 tbsp (30 ml) fresh lime juice

Salt and pepper

¼ cup (12 g) chopped chives, for garnish

Add the avocado, cucumber, scallion, broth, coconut milk and lime juice to a blender. Blend until smooth. Season the soup with salt and pepper to taste. Serve with chopped chives.

PER 1 CUP (240 ML) SERVING WITHOUT GARNISHES: CALORIES 291 ⟫⟫ FAT 27.8 G ⟫⟫ CARBOHYDRATES 9.8 G ⟫⟫ FIBER 4.7 G ⟫⟫ PROTEIN 4.9 G

GRILLED CORN AND TOMATO SOUP WITH GUACAMOLE

MAKES 1 QUART (950 ML)

Grilling the corn and tomatoes is what makes this recipe. Leftover grilled corn from a barbecue works perfectly here. Quickly grilling the tomatoes just takes a few minutes but does wonders taste-wise.

6 ears corn, shucked (should equal roughly 3 cups [450 g] of kernels), divided

2 tsp (10 ml) olive oil, plus more for brushing

2 tomatoes, ripe but firm

1 yellow onion, diced

3 cloves garlic, minced

1 tsp chipotle chili powder or cayenne

4 cups (960 ml) vegetable broth

1 cup (240 ml) unsweetened almond milk

Salt and pepper

Vegan Sour Cream (page 180), for garnish

GUACAMOLE

1 avocado

2 tbsp (2 g) chopped, fresh cilantro leaves and stems

2 tsp (10 ml) fresh lime juice

1 small red onion, finely diced

¼ tsp salt

Start your grill or heat up a grill pan. Brush each shucked ear of corn with olive oil. Place the corn over direct heat on a medium-hot grill. Grill the corn for roughly 10 minutes. Keep a close eye on the corn and rotate it every few minutes. Remove the corn from the grill once they are lightly browned and set aside.

Cut the tomatoes in half. Brush any seeds and pulp gently away with your fingers. Brush the cut side of the tomatoes with olive oil. It's best to grill tomatoes on a grill pan. Grill the tomatoes, cut side down, over direct high heat. Cover the grill and cook for 2 to 4 minutes. Place the tomatoes on a plate and set aside.

Heat 2 teaspoons (10 ml) of olive oil in a large pot. Add the onion and cook for 5 minutes. Once the corn has cooled enough, cut the kernels off the cobs. Set ½ cup (72 g) of corn kernels aside to be used as garnish later. Add the corn, tomatoes, garlic, chili powder and broth. Bring the soup to a boil over high heat, then reduce heat and simmer for 10 minutes.

Once the vegetables are tender, use an immersion blender to purée the soup, or blend the soup in batches in a blender. Return the soup to the pot and stir in the almond milk. Let the soup simmer for 5 minutes to thicken. Season the soup with salt and pepper to taste.

Prepare the guacamole by mashing the avocado flesh in a bowl with a fork. Add the chopped cilantro, lime juice, onion and salt. Add additional salt to taste.

Ladle the soup into bowls and top with a dollop of guacamole, vegan sour cream and some reserved corn kernels.

PER 1 CUP (240 ML) SERVING WITHOUT GARNISHES: CALORIES 244 ⫸ FAT 6.9 G ⫸ CARBOHYDRATES 40.0 G ⫸ FIBER 6.5 G ⫸ PROTEIN 11.8 G

EXTRAS AND TOPPINGS

Soups are always delicious, but sometimes they need a great topping or two to make them extra special. A dollop of Vegan Sour Cream (page 180) or a few Homemade Croutons (page 184) can really make a difference.

This chapter features just a few of my favorite toppings. The most important recipe in this chapter though is for Homemade Vegetable Broth (page 187). Learning how to make your own broth will really step up your soup-making game to a whole new level.

VEGAN SOUR CREAM

MAKES 1½ CUPS (181 G)

Making your own dairy-free sour cream couldn't be easier. Add a dollop on
top of any of your favorite soups for an extra creamy texture. Note: The longer you soak your cashews, the creamier
the sour cream will be. Overnight is ideal.

1 cup (150 g) raw cashews, soaked for at least 1 hour

¼ cup (12 g) nutritional yeast

1 tbsp (15 ml) fresh lemon juice

1 tsp apple cider vinegar

½ tsp salt

¼ cup (60 ml) water, plus more if needed

Place all of the ingredients in a food processor or high-powered blender. Pulse and blend until smooth, adding more water until the desired consistency is achieved. Keep the sour cream in the refrigerator in an airtight container and use within three days.

PER ¼ CUP (50 G) SERVING: CALORIES 156 ❯❯❯❱ FAT 10.9 G ❯❯❯❱ CARBOHYDRATES 10.6 G ❯❯❯❱ FIBER 2.4 G ❯❯❯❱ PROTEIN 6.6 G

WHIPPED COCONUT CREAM

MAKES 1¼ CUPS (151 G)

Whipped coconut cream is incredibly easy to make. I use it not only as a soup topping, but also for desserts.

1 (13.5-oz [400-ml]) can full-fat coconut milk

Place the can of coconut milk in the back of your fridge and leave it there overnight. The next day, carefully remove the can from the fridge. Try not to slosh it around. Open the can. You'll notice that there will be hard, white coconut cream on top and the clear coconut water will have settled on the bottom of the can.

Scoop the hard white coconut cream out of the can and place it in a bowl. Beat the coconut cream with a hand mixer on high speed for 5 to 8 minutes until stiff peaks form.

Use the whipped coconut cream immediately, or store it in an airtight container in the fridge and use within two days.

PER ⅛ CUP (30 ML): CALORIES 93 ❯❯❯❱ FAT 9.7 G ❯❯❯❱ CARBOHYDRATES 2.3 G ❯❯❯❱ FIBER 0.9 G ❯❯❯❱ PROTEIN 0.9 G

BASIL WALNUT PESTO

MAKES 1½ CUPS (181 G)

Homemade pestos are simple to make, cheaper and taste much fresher than their store-bought counterparts. This basil and walnut pesto is a recipe I make at least once a week. We use it for pasta, sandwiches and as a delicious soup topping.

1 cup (30 g) tightly packed basil leaves

½ cup (60 g) walnuts

1 clove garlic

¼ to ½ cup (60 to 120 ml) olive oil

Salt to taste

Pulse all of the ingredients in a food processor until your desired consistency is achieved.

*See photo on page 178.

PER 1 TABLESPOON (15 G) SERVING: CALORIES 36 ⋙ FAT 3.9 G ⋙ CARBOHYDRATES 0.3 G ⋙ FIBER 0.2 G ⋙ PROTEIN 0.7 G

ALMOND KALE PESTO

MAKES 1½ CUPS (181 G)

Making your own pesto has the benefit that you can play around with different herbs, greens, nuts and seeds. This almond and kale pesto quickly became one of my favorite combos.

½ cup (80 g) almonds

1 tightly packed cup (50 g) kale, stems removed

2 cloves garlic

¼ cup (12 g) nutritional yeast

¼ to ½ cup (60 to 120 ml) olive oil

Salt to taste

Pulse the almonds, kale, garlic and nutritional yeast in a food processor until the almonds and kale are slightly chunky. Stir the olive oil in with a spoon, adding more if needed. Add salt to taste.

PER 1 TABLESPOON (15 G) SERVING: CALORIES 42 ⋙ FAT 4.1 G ⋙ CARBOHYDRATES 1.2 G ⋙ FIBER 0.6 G ⋙ PROTEIN 1 G

HOMEMADE VEGETABLE BROTH POWDER

MAKES ⅓ CUP (45 G) (ENOUGH FOR 10 CUPS [2.4 L] VEGETABLE BROTH)

I love having this vegetable broth powder around. It works the same way you would use bouillon cubes.

This is a rough guideline. Add other ingredients and play around with it until you find the right combo for you.

Broth powder is usually very salty. Depending on how much you add, it will vary on how much you'll need to add to make your vegetable broth. This recipe will equal to 1 tablespoon (12 g) for every 2 cups (473 ml) of water to make 2 cups (473 ml) of vegetable broth.

1 yellow onion

1 large carrot

2 ribs celery

⅓ cup (10 g) fresh parsley

1 scallion

2 tsp (10 g) salt

½ tsp turmeric

¼ tsp ginger

¼ tsp nutmeg

Preheat your oven to 175°F (80°C).

Finely dice the yellow onion, and grate the carrot and celery as fine as possible. Chop the parsley and scallion into small slices. Spread the onion, carrot, celery, parsley and scallion on an unlined baking sheet and place in the oven.

After 40 minutes, carefully stir the vegetables around and bake for another 60 minutes. By then, the vegetable should be very dry.

Turn the oven off at this point, but leave the pan in the oven for another 2 hours, or overnight, to allow the vegetables to dry even further. Remove the pan from the oven and let it sit out for one day before pulsing it in a food processor until it is pulverized.

Mix the pulverized powder together with the salt, turmeric, ginger and nutmeg. This is your finished vegetable broth powder!

PER 1 TABLESPOON (12 G) SERVING: CALORIES 19 ⇒⇒⇒ FAT 0.1 G ⇒⇒⇒ CARBOHYDRATES 4.3 G ⇒⇒⇒ FIBER 1.2 G ⇒⇒⇒ PROTEIN 0.6 G

HOMEMADE CROUTONS

MAKES 2 CUPS (200 G)

It's best to use day-old or even two-day-old bread with a nice crust for croutons.
Once you've started making your own croutons, you won't bother buying them ever again.

3 slices bread

Olive oil

Salt

Fresh cracked pepper

Garlic powder

Dried rosemary (alternatively, you can use any other dried herb you have)

Dice the bread into cubes. The size of these cubes doesn't matter. Put the bread cubes in a bowl and drizzle the bread with a little bit of olive oil. The amount of olive oil you use will vary on how much and the type of bread you use. Each cube should have just a tiny bit of olive oil on it. They should not be covered or soaked in oil.

Start off by adding a pinch of salt and pepper and the garlic powder and rosemary. Use a spoon to mix everything together. Add more olive oil if you notice that some bread cubes are very dry. Add more salt, pepper, garlic powder and rosemary if needed.

Heat a frying pan over medium-high heat and add the bread cubes. The bread should be in the frying pan in a single layer. If your frying pan isn't large enough, make the croutons in batches instead of overcrowding them.

Cook the croutons for at least 10 minutes, letting each crouton sit for a minute in the pan to allow it become golden before turning it. The best way to ensure each side is evenly cooked is to use tongs instead of a turner spatula. Once the croutons are golden and crisp, remove them from the pan and use them within three days.

FRESH GARLIC CILANTRO SALSA

MAKES 1 CUP (160 G)

When in doubt, make your own salsa! It's not just great for chips, but also as a soup topping.
It's exceptionally great on the Loaded Taco Soup (page 154).

2 cloves garlic

1 cup (16 g) fresh cilantro, stems and leaves

1 small red onion

1 tomato

1 tbsp (15 ml) fresh lime juice

¼ tsp salt

Pulse all of the ingredients together in a food processor. Season the salsa with more salt if needed.

PER 2 TABLESPOON (20 G) SERVING: CALORIES 10 ⟫⟫ FAT 0.1 G ⟫⟫ CARBOHYDRATES 2.1 G ⟫⟫ FIBER 0.6 G ⟫⟫ PROTEIN 0.4 G

VEGAN CHEDDAR CHEESE SAUCE

MAKES 1 CUP (200 G)

Words can't describe how much I love this vegan cheddar cheese sauce made with real ingredients. Try it in my
Broccoli "Cheddar" Soup (page 66) and on top of the Loaded Taco Soup (page 154).

8 oz (226 g) carrots

⅛ cup (35 g) coconut oil, not melted

4 tbsp (60 ml) unsweetened almond milk

¼ cup (12 g) nutritional yeast

1 tbsp (15 ml) lemon juice

2 tsp (10 ml) Dijon mustard, optional

1 tsp paprika

¼ tsp garlic powder

¼ tsp salt

If possible, steam your carrots using a steamer basket for 5 to 10 minutes until they are tender. The time will vary depending on how large and thick your carrots are. If you can't steam your carrots, boil them in hot water. The boil time can also vary greatly. Your carrots will be tender and ready once you can easily pierce them with a fork.

Put the cooked carrots in a food processor along with the remaining ingredients and pulse/blend until smooth.

Use the cheese sauce right away, or store it in an airtight container in the fridge. The coconut oil will make the cheese sauce hard in the fridge, so be sure to slowly reheat it on the stove or in the microwave before using again.

PER ¼ CUP (50 G) SERVING: CALORIES 117 ⟫⟫ FAT 9.3 G ⟫⟫ CARBOHYDRATES 7.8 G ⟫⟫ FIBER 2.6 G ⟫⟫ PROTEIN 2.2 G

HOMEMADE VEGETABLE BROTH

MAKES 2 QUARTS (1.9 L)

A great stock is really what makes all the difference in a soup. This is a basic stock recipe. However, the best vegetable stocks are usually made with kitchen scraps. I like to keep a zip-top bag in my fridge where I toss carrot and leek greens, squash peels and wilted herbs. Check the list below for which ingredients should and shouldn't be used to make stock and then create your own! If you are using your own vegetable broth, always season your soups with salt while cooking.

2 onions

2 leeks

4 ribs celery

3 to 4 carrots

8 sprigs parsley

4 sprigs thyme

2 bay leaves

1 tsp peppercorns

4 quarts (3.8 L) water

Wash all the vegetable ingredients and place them in a large pot. Cover the ingredients with the water. Heat the pot over medium-high heat. Once the pot starts boiling, reduce the heat to medium-low and simmer, uncovered, for an hour. Stir the vegetables in the pot every 10 to 15 minutes.

If available, line your strainer with cheesecloth. Remove the vegetables from the pot and strain the broth. Add the used vegetables to your compost, if you have one.

Store the broth in airtight containers in the fridge. Use the broth within a week.

You can also freeze your vegetable broth. It can keep up to six months this way.

Vegetables to use:
- Carrots
- Parsnips
- Celeriac
- Celery
- Onion
- Leeks
- Mushrooms
- Herbs
- Fennel
- Tomatoes
- Squash peels
- Okra
- Scallions
- Shallots

Vegetables not to use:
- Garlic
- Potatoes
- Radishes
- Rutabagas
- Sweet potatoes
- Turnips
- Green beans
- Beets
- Cabbages
- Watercress
- Brussels sprouts
- Bitter greens
- Zucchini
- Turnips
- Corn
- Kohlrabi
- Broccoli
- Cauliflower

ACKNOWLEDGMENTS

My wonderful blog readers are the ones who deserve the biggest thank you. You inspired me to become more creative in the kitchen and a better photographer. Without my blog readers, I wouldn't be able to turn my passion into a career and for that I am forever grateful.

I can't possibly thank my husband, Max, and my sons, Daniel and Phillip, enough for eating a colossal amount of soup throughout the process of making this cookbook. Your support, love and brutally honest feedback are what kept me going.

Thanks to my little sister, Rebecca, for being incredibly helpful and always giving me words of encouragement.

Last but definitely not least, thank you to all the wonderful people at Page Street Publishing who made this cookbook possible. Especially Elizabeth, who helped me throughout the entire process and was also quick to answer any questions I had, and Meg, whose design work I am in awe of.

ABOUT THE AUTHOR

Vanessa Croessmann is the creator of the popular vegan food blog, VeganFamilyRecipes.com. She spends most of her time pursuing her passion of creating and photographing healthy, plant-based recipes for her many readers around the world. She lives in Germany with her husband and two children.

INDEX